The Subprime Solution

Robert J. Shiller

THE Subprime SOLUTION

How Today's Global Financial Crisis Happened, and What to Do about It

Princeton University Press   PRINCETON AND OXFORD

The author is the Arthur M. Okun Professor of Economics at the Cowles
Foundation for Research in Economics and Professor of Finance at the
International Center for Finance, Yale University; research associate at the
National Bureau of Economic Research; and co-founder and principal of two
U.S. firms that are in the business of issuing securities: MacroMarkets LLC
and Macro Financial LLC. The views expressed herein are solely those of the
author and do not necessarily reflect the views of these institutions.

Published by Princeton University Press, 41 William Street, Princeton,
New Jersey 08540

In the United Kingdom: Princeton University Press, 6 Oxford Street,
Woodstock, Oxfordshire OX20 1TW

Library of Congress Cataloging-in-Publication Data

Shiller, Robert J.
    The subprime solution : how today's global financial crisis happened,
and what to do about it / Robert J. Shiller.
      p. cm.
    Includes index.
    ISBN 978-0-691-13929-6 (hbk. : alk. paper)
    1. Mortgage loans. 2. Secondary mortgage market. 3. Real estate
investment. 4. Financial crises. I. Title.
    HG2040.15.S45   2008
    332.7'22—dc22   2008013734

British Library Cataloging-in-Publication Data is available

This book has been composed in Minion

Printed on acid-free paper. ∞

press.princeton.edu

Printed in the United States of America

10 9 8 7 6 5 4

A general bonfire is so great a necessity that unless
we can make of it an orderly and good-tempered affair
in which no serious injustice is done to anyone, it will,
when it comes at last, grow into a conflagration that
may destroy much else as well.

—John Maynard Keynes

The Economic Consequences of the Peace, 1919

Contents

Acknowledgments

I am profoundly grateful for the guidance of Peter Dougherty, director of Princeton University Press, who had the inspiration to see how ideas I had expressed about the current financial crisis could be developed further and woven together into a short book. As I wrote this book, I found myself reflecting on the work of the late Franco Modigliani, my first mentor, who taught me about social purpose in economics. Ideas came too from George Akerlof, for we have been writing together a book about animal spirits and the economy, which will appear soon. Others to whom I owe gratitude for help with this book include Sara Greenberg, Jessica Jeffers, Bjorn Johnson, Richard Kadlick, Terry Loebs, Daniel Luskin, Arthur Nacht, Jonathan Reiss, John Shiller, T. N. Srinivasan, Ronit Walny, and

James Warrick-Alexander. I could not have written this book in a timely manner without the devoted support of my assistant Carol Copeland. Finally, I am indebted to my wife, Virginia Shiller, for her patience and emotional support, as well as her intellectual contributions to my work through the three decades of our marriage.

The Subprime Solution

Introduction

The *subprime crisis* is the name for what is a historic turning point in our economy and our culture. It is, at its core, the result of a speculative bubble in the housing market that began to burst in the United States in 2006 and has now caused ruptures across many other countries in the form of financial failures and a global credit crunch. The forces unleashed by the subprime crisis will probably run rampant for years, threatening more and more collateral damage. The disruption in our credit markets is already of historic proportions and will have important economic impacts. More importantly, this crisis has set in motion fundamental societal changes—changes that affect our consumer habits, our values, our relatedness to each other. From now on we will all be conducting our lives and doing business with each other a little bit differently.

Allowing these destructive changes to proceed un-
impeded could cause damage not only to the economy
but to the social fabric—the trust and optimism people
feel for each other and for their shared institutions and
ways of life—for decades to come. The social fabric itself
is so hard to measure that it is easily overlooked in favor of smaller, more discrete, elements and details. But
the social fabric is indeed at risk and should be central
to our attention as we respond to the subprime crisis.

History proves the importance of economic policies
for preserving the social fabric. Europe after World War
I was seriously damaged by one peculiar economic arrangement: the Treaty of Versailles. The treaty, which
ended the war, imposed on Germany punitive reparations far beyond its ability to pay. John Maynard Keynes
resigned in protest from the British delegation at Versailles and, in 1919, wrote *The Economic Consequences of
the Peace,* which predicted that the treaty would result in
disaster. Keynes was largely ignored, the treaty remained
in force, and indeed Germany never was able to pay the
penalties imposed. The intense resentment caused by the
treaty was one of the factors that led, a generation later,
to World War II.

A comparable disaster—albeit one not of quite the
same magnitude—is brewing today, as similar concerns
are hammering at our psyches. Once again, many people,

unable to repay their debts, are being pursued aggressively by creditors. Once again, they often feel that the situation is not of their own making, but the product of forces beyond their control. Once again, they see once-trusted economic institutions collapsing around them. Once again, they feel that they were lied to—fed overly optimistic stories that encouraged them to take excessive risks.

It is impossible to predict the nature and extent of the damage that the current economic and social dysphoria and disorder will create. But a good part of it will likely be measured in slower economic growth for years to come. We may well experience several years of a bad economy, as occurred, for example, after the profligate mortgage lending booms in both Sweden and Mexico in the early 1990s. There could even be another "lost decade," like that suffered by Mexico in the 1980s after its spending spree during the oil price boom, or by Japan in the 1990s after the bursting of the 1980s bubble in its stock and housing markets.

In this book I argue that the housing bubble that created the subprime crisis ultimately grew as big as it did because we as a society do not understand, or know how to deal with, speculative bubbles. Even intelligent, well-informed people—who certainly knew that there had been bubbles throughout history and could even recite examples—typically did not comprehend that an epidemic of irrational public enthusiasm for housing investments was the core of the problem. Business and government leaders did not know how to deal with this situation, nor did they establish the kinds of new financial institutions that could have managed it.

The view that the ultimate cause of the global financial crisis is the psychology of the real estate bubble (with contributions from the stock market bubble before that) has certainly been expressed before. But it would appear that most people have not taken this view to heart, and at the very least that they do not appreciate all of its ramifications. Accounts of the crisis often seem instead to place the ultimate blame entirely on such factors as growing dishonesty among mortgage lenders; increasing greed among securitizers, hedge funds, and rating agencies; or the mistakes of former Federal Reserve chairman Alan Greenspan.

It is time to recognize what has been happening and to take fundamental steps to restructure the institutional foundations of the housing and financial economy. This means taking both short-run steps to alleviate the crisis and making longer-term changes that will inhibit the development of bubbles, stabilize the housing and larger financial markets, and provide greater financial security to households and businesses, all the while allowing new ideas to drive financial innovation.

A Crisis in a Bubble

By now the whole world has heard the story of the problems in the subprime mortgage market, which began to show up in the United States in 2007 and then spread to other countries. Home prices and homeownership had been booming since the late 1990s, and investing in a house had seemed a sure route to financial security and even wealth.

U.S. homeownership rates rose over the period 1997–2005 for all regions, all age groups, all racial groups, and all income groups. According to the U.S. Census, the homeownership rate increased from 65.7% to 68.9% (which represents an 11.5% increase in the number of owner-occupied homes) over that period. The increases in homeownership were largest in the West, for those under the age of 35, for those with below-median incomes, and for Hispanics and blacks.

Encouraging homeownership is a worthy and admirable national goal. It conveys a sense of participation and belonging, and high homeownership rates are beneficial to a healthy society. Later in this chapter I trace the evolution of the systems put in place in the United States in the twentieth century to promote homeownership. But the subprime housing dilemma in the United States points up problems with over-promoting homeownership. Homeownership, for all its advantages, is not the ideal housing arrangement for all people in all circumstances. And we are now coming to appreciate the reality of this, for the homeownership rate has been falling in the United States since 2005.

What was the chain of events in the subprime crisis? Overly aggressive mortgage lenders, compliant appraisers, and complacent borrowers proliferated to feed the housing boom. Mortgage originators, who planned to sell off the mortgages to securitizers, stopped worrying about repayment risk. They typically made only perfunctory efforts to assess borrowers' ability to repay their loans—often failing to verify borrowers' income with the Internal Revenue Service, even if they possessed signed authorization forms permitting them to do so. Sometimes these lenders enticed the naïve, with poor credit histories, to borrow in the ballooning subprime mortgage market. These mortgages were packaged, sold, and resold in sophisticated but arcane ways to investors around the world, setting the stage for a crisis of truly global proportions. The housing bubble, combined with the incentive system implicit in the securitization process, amplified moral hazard, further emboldening some of the worst actors among mortgage lenders.

High home prices made it profitable to build homes, and the share of residential investment in U.S. gross domestic product (GDP) rose to 6.3% in the fourth quarter of 2005, the highest level since the pre–Korean War housing boom of 1950–51. The huge supply of new homes began to glut the market, and, despite the optimistic outlooks of national leaders, U.S. home prices began to fall in mid-2006. As prices declined at an accelerating rate, the boom in home construction collapsed.

At the same time, mortgage rates began to reset to higher levels after initial "teaser" periods ended. Borrowers, particularly subprime borrowers, began defaulting, often owing more than their homes were worth or unable to support their higher monthly payments with current incomes. Now many of the financial institutions that participated in what once seemed a brave new world of expanding homeownership and exotic financial innovation are in varying degrees of distress. The world's credit markets have shown symptoms of locking up.

We may be in for a severe economic contraction that could create hardship for millions of people, spreading far beyond the subprime borrowers at the center of the crisis. Major losses occurred in U.S. banks and brokerage firms. The heads of Citibank, Merrill Lynch, and Morgan Stanley lost their jobs. The situation remains critical. The crisis has bled over to other sectors besides housing. Credit card and automobile loan defaults have been ominously increasing. The credit ratings of municipal bond insurers are being downgraded, creating a risk that the problem will spread to state and local government financing. The market for commercial paper has suffered a severe shock, and the market for corporate loan obligations appears troubled as well.

Nor did the subprime crisis end at America's borders. Booming real estate markets have shown signs of peaking, or at least of flattening out, in many countries. The effects of the financial crisis have also filtered into other countries, as witnessed by the failures of IKB Deutsche Industriebank AG, SachsenLB, WestLB, and BayernLB in Germany, the failure of funds sponsored by BNP Paribas in France, and the run on the Northern Rock Building Society in the United Kingdom.

Then again, these problems from outside the United States have fed back into the country, manifested in a declining dollar, a faltering stock market, and more financial failures, notably that of the venerable U.S. investment bank Bear Stearns. This grim feedback loop—with problems moving from the United States to the rest of the world and back again to the United States—has certainly not yet run its course.

The same feedback seems also at this date to be contributing to a global energy crisis and a global food crisis. Speculative enthusiasm has helped push oil prices to record levels, stimulating a demand for ethanol for fuel from grains, thus reducing the supply of grains for food. Prices of grains are shooting up so high that poor people have difficulty staving off hunger.

The same kind of speculative thinking that has propelled the stock market and housing market in the recent past seems to be at work in these markets as well. The nations of the world have had difficulty protecting themselves from these crises. A number of less developed countries have tried to protect themselves from the global food crisis by putting export controls on food grains. But they have found that such controls do not work, since prices of grains within their borders stay high after such controls, as speculative hoarding within the country responds to the high world food prices and withdraws supply from local markets. Speculative instability in the market for food may eventually result in price breaks there, but one shudders to think of the human consequences until it does.

Mend It, Don't End It

The current financial crisis is often viewed as a reason to sound retreat—to return to yesterday's simpler methods of financial dealing. This would be a mistake. On the contrary, the current situation is *really* an opportunity to redouble our efforts to rethink and improve our risk-management institutions, the framework that undergirds our increasingly sophisticated financial sector. Despite the present crisis, modern finance has produced historic achievements in recent decades and serves as a powerful engine of economic growth, from underwriting new businesses in the private sector to supporting vital research in the universities to building schools and hospitals in the public sector.

Every crisis contains the seeds of change. Now is the time to restructure the institutional firmament of financial activity in positive ways that will stabilize the economy, rekindle the wealth of nations, reinforce the best of financial innovation, and leave society much better off than if there had not been such a crisis.

This book is an effort to explain the current subprime crisis and lay the foundation for such an institutional rebirth. It suggests both commonsense short-run fixes and deeper long-term improvements that will serve us into the indefinite future. The book cannot consider all the proposals and counterproposals that others have offered to deal with the crisis—there are simply too many of them. But it will set forth the greater goals around which future solutions might cluster.

The book is intended for readers in countries all over the world. The subprime crisis is now a truly international event, and the solutions offered here can generally be adapted to other countries as well. As already noted, institutional reform means providing a stronger framework within which our real estate and financial markets can operate. No matter how powerful and technologically sophisticated the train, it is only as good as the track on which it runs. Regulatory and insurance institutions are the track that carries our financial and real estate markets. But these existing risk-management institutions are old and unstable. We are running bullet trains on ancient track. Our leaders in government and in business must overhaul and replace the rails and ties. The subprime solution is all about institutional reform: the vision to see beyond short-term fixes and the courage to undertake reform at the highest levels.

Lessons from the Last Big Housing Crisis

While the implications of the subprime crisis are global, the crisis itself must be understood in its place and time of origin, twentieth-century America. Before the current problem, the last major housing crisis in the United States took place in 1925–33. Home prices fell a total of 30% over this interval, and the unemployment rate rose to 25% at the peak of the Great Depression. The crisis revealed glaring defects in the financial institutions of the period. At that time most people borrowed with short-term mortgages of five years or less, which they expected to roll over shortly before they came due. As the crisis took hold, borrowers increasingly found that they were unable to refinance their mortgages, and so they stood to lose their homes.

No public institutions were in place at the time to prevent borrowers from being evicted from their homes owing to their inability to secure new mortgages. But because concerted efforts were made by leaders to change the institutional framework, mass evictions were avoided and recovery was eventually achieved.

The policy responses to that historical crisis are an inspiration for the kind of solutions that should be promoted to address the current crisis. As the housing problems of the Depression era worsened, major innovations appeared in the private and public sectors. While history has emphasized the importance of Franklin Delano Roosevelt's New Deal, the significant changes were not simply the result of one man's policies. Rather, they reflected an effort, involving leaders from government and business alike, to try to understand the crisis and change the institutional infrastructure of the U.S. economy.

The National Association of Real Estate Boards, a precursor to today's National Association of Realtors, proposed in the early 1930s that Congress create a new home-loan banking system, parallel to the Federal Reserve System that had been legislated in 1913. Just as the Federal Reserve System had twelve regional banks, so too did the new Federal Home Loan Bank System. Just as the Federal Reserve System had the power to discount assets of its member banks, so too could the Federal Home Loan Bank System provide the same help to mortgage originators. This was large-scale thinking in response to a large-scale crisis. The Federal Home Loan Bank System has since been modified, but it is still with us today, providing assistance during the current crisis by supplying funding for mortgages.

Private-sector reforms were equally innovative. In 1932 the real estate appraisal industry pulled itself together to become a truly professional organization with the founding of the American Institute of Real Estate Appraisers, whose successor today is the Appraisal Institute. It was not formally called the Appraisal Institute until it merged with the Society of Real Estate Appraisers in 1991. Yet by the early 1930s its accredited members were already putting the initials M.A.I., for "Member,

Appraisal Institute," after their names as a credential. Under the pressure of the crisis, the newly professionalized appraisal industry began taking advantage of the latest developments in information technology, processing data on a large scale using punched cards and computing systems produced by Remington Rand and the International Business Machines Corporation. The improvements that originated in the private sector during the housing crisis of the 1930s have continued to the present day, helping prevent—or at least limit—further crises by providing a more secure valuation of homes for mortgage lenders.

A landmark change occurred on the legislative front as well, in response to the crush of foreclosures against homeowners. The U.S. Congress approved a new bankruptcy law in 1933, near the end of the administration of Herbert Hoover, which made it possible for the first time for most ordinary wage earners to avail themselves of bankruptcy protection. Thus the crisis led to reforms that not only stabilized the housing sector but further democratized the financial institutions of the day, creating public goods that made more effective financial technology available to everyone.

The reforms did not stop there. In 1933, with Roosevelt as the new president, Congress created the Home Owners' Loan Corporation (HOLC), which lent to local

home-financing institutions, taking risky home mortgages as collateral, and thereby provided a government
subsidy to home mortgages. But the HOLC did more
than simply provide a subsidy: the organization changed
the very standards of the mortgage industry. The HOLC
insisted that the new mortgages it sponsored be fifteen-
year loans that were both fixed-rate and self-amortizing,
that is, that were paid off by steady monthly payments
with no large payments due at maturity.

In 1934 Congress created the Federal Housing Administration (FHA), which was intended to promote homeownership among those who could not then afford homes.
The FHA went even further than the HOLC in improving
the institution of mortgages, raising maturities to twenty
years and also requiring, as did the HOLC, that mortgages
be fixed-rate and self-amortizing. This began a trend to
the familiar fixed-rate mortgage of today; starting in the
1950s, mortgages began to be thirty-year instruments,
again with FHA encouragement.

Also in 1934 Congress created the Federal Deposit
Insurance Corporation, which insured our banking
system against the kind of terrible collapse that had occurred in 1933 in connection with the housing crisis. Deposit insurance on a national scale was a radical new idea
then; it has served us very well, and there has not been
another bank run in the United States since.

A further innovation introduced in 1934 was the creation by Congress of the Securities and Exchange Commission (SEC), a regulatory agency that was dedicated from the start to making financial markets work. The SEC has dealt constructively with the financial community, doing its job in a way that is fair and useful to all parties.

In 1938 Congress created the Federal National Mortgage Association, later nicknamed (and now officially renamed) Fannie Mae, which further supported the mortgage industry and eventually fostered the widespread securitization of mortgages.

The soundness of the ideas implemented in response to the financial crisis of the 1930s is evident in the durability of the institutions created: all but the HOLC are still in existence. Moreover, these institutions have become models for similar institutions the world over. While it took many years, and often decades, for some of these institutional models to be disseminated across the globe, every country with developed economic institutions now has the equivalent of the SEC, some such organizations having been established as recently as the 1990s. Virtually every major country of the world also has deposit insurance for its banks and institutions to encourage homeownership for those with lower incomes.

Band-Aids for a Burst Bubble: Today's Response

Despite the severity of the current subprime crisis, the response by government today has been disappointingly limited relative to that in the 1930s, and totally inadequate given the scope of the problem.

The FHASecure bailouts announced by President George W. Bush in the summer of 2007 were supposed to help borrowers whose adjustable-rate mortgages were resetting at prohibitively high rates. But as of mid 2008 the total FHASecure refinancing amounted to less than 2% of the single-family guaranty book of business of that 1930s legacy, Fannie Mae.

The Master Liquidity Enhancement Conduit (MLEC) "Super S.I.V." rescue plan, proposed in the fall of 2007 by U.S. Treasury Secretary Henry M. Paulson Jr., would have been, at maximum, less than a tenth the size of the Federal Home Loan Bank System that fortunately is still with us from Great Depression reforms. As it turned out, the MLEC was canceled altogether.

The standards for adjustable-rate mortgage resets promoted by the American Securitization Forum in 2007 will result in mortgage payment adjustments less than 1% of the deposits insured by that 1934 creation, the Federal Deposit Insurance Corporation.

The Project Lifeline extensions of time before foreclosure that the Bush administration announced it had
negotiated in February 2008 were only a thirty-day extension of the time to failure. All this amounted to but
a statement of intent on the part of major lenders in response to the president's calls for action.

Other measures taken include interest rate cuts by
the Federal Reserve; the Term Auction Facility (TAF),
announced December 21, 2007; the Term Securities
Lending Facility (TSLF), announced March 11, 2008;
and its Primary Dealer Credit Facility (PDCF), announced March 16, 2008, as well as the passage of the
Economic Stimulus Act of 2008, signed into law by
President Bush on February 13, 2008. Although perhaps helpful, the tax rebates in the stimulus package,
and the total size of the TAF, TSLF, and PDCF loans
altogether have so far been on the order of only a half a
percent of U.S. household assets; while they have been
increasing, they are still not up to the magnitude of the
problem. Even if their scope were greatly expanded, we
do not know that any of these specific measures would
do much to solve the fundamental crisis of confidence
that lies at the heart of the subprime crisis.*

---

*Some have argued that the TAF should have no effect on the overall
level of confidence in our financial institutions as measured by interest
rate spreads, and in fact there has been no consistent effect. See John B.

None of these proposals represents a true institutional innovation that would create a better environment to support our real estate and financial markets. They are all merely quick fixes that fail to address the full scope of the problem.

The U.S. Congress has been slow to react to the crisis. U.S. Senator Charles Schumer (D-NY), at a 2007 Joint Economic Committee hearing at which I was a witness, said, "I fear that we still don't appreciate the seriousness of the problem we are facing. Our policy responses are not matching the magnitude of the risk that still lies ahead."* That was some months before this writing, and the Fed and Congress have since paid more focused attention to the crisis, but it is still unclear that they are going to be effective in committing the substantial resources the situation demands. As the crisis worsens and begins to consume significant amounts of government resources, they may simply not be able to keep up. The steps taken so far have been ad hoc, and unlike the 1930s nothing fundamental is being done.

Taylor and John C. Williams, "A Black Swan in the Money Market," Federal Reserve Bank of San Francisco, April 2008, http://www.frbsf.org/publications/economics/papers/2008/wp08-04bk.pdf.

*Charles E. Schumer, "Opening Statement," Joint Economic Committee Hearing, "Evolution of an Economic Crisis? The Subprime Lending Disaster and the Threat to the Broader Economy," September 19, 2007, p. 2, http://jec.senate.gov.

Framing Institutional Reform for the Future

Reporters repeatedly ask me what I think is the probability of a protracted recession spurred by the subprime crisis. Only rarely do they ask me what I think should be done to solve the fundamental problems highlighted by the subprime crisis, or inquire about how we could set up new or reformed institutions that might help insulate our society against the fundamental problems that underlie the crisis. But these are *exactly* the questions we should be asking ourselves. A plan to dramatically reduce our vulnerability to financial crises like the current subprime crisis would rest on two principles.

In the immediate short run, government and business leaders must deal with the problem created by the bubble and its aftermath. The ship is sinking, and we have to save it before we do anything else. In fact, we have to bail out some people who have fared particularly badly, and we also have to arrange bailouts in certain extreme cases to prevent failure of our economic system. These bailouts must be done promptly and correctly, so that they do not come across as unjust or unfair. This situation also calls for a short-term government intervention designed to shore up those mortgages that are teetering on the edge of default, perhaps modeled after the Home Owners' Loan Corporation of the 1930s.

In the longer run, as noted above, we need to develop stronger risk-management institutions to inhibit the growth of bubbles—the root cause of events such as the current subprime crisis—and to better enable the members of our society to insulate themselves against them when they do develop.

This proposed subprime solution means embracing the following goals:

First, improving the financial information infrastructure so that the greatest number of people can avail themselves of sound financial practices, products, and services. This means delivering enhanced financial information, better financial advice, and greater consumer protection to larger segments of society, and also implementing an improved system of economic units of measurement. These steps will set the necessary groundwork, so that all consumers and households can make financial decisions based on the best possible intelligence rather than rules of thumb or, worse still, mere whimsy. Better financial information and decision making would, by themselves, check the incidence of bubbles.

Second, extending the scope of financial markets to cover a wider array of economic risks. Such an initiative would include, in the first instance, vastly expanded markets for handling real estate risk such as the new futures markets in Chicago, and also markets for other vital economic risks as well. These broader markets, coupled with a more sound information infrastructure, would provide the financial foundation for a variety of new initiatives that would help to inhibit the growth of bubbles.

Third, creating retail financial instruments—including continuous-workout mortgages, and home equity insurance—to provide greater security to consumers. Today the typical household has as its principal investment its home. A home represents a highly leveraged exposure to a single, stationary plot of real estate—about the riskiest asset one can imagine. The standard mortgage provides no protection against difficulties in repaying the lender due to changes in the marketplace. But mortgages can and should be designed to compensate for these changes by including provisions to ensure homeowners against their major risks. Other retail institutions can protect those who have paid off their mortgages, and they can protect non-homeowners from economic contractions as well.

If we work toward these goals, we would not only curb the creation of the bubbles that fuel crises such as today's subprime disaster but also afford greater protection against risks, encourage better financial behavior and enhanced household wealth, strengthen the social fabric, and create the conditions for greater economic stability and growth.

Implementing these and other important institutional changes in all their detail is a tall order. But this is a project for leaders from all segments of society, not merely a president's or a prime minister's inner circle. It will require the combined efforts of policy makers, business executives, the media, and academics. Fortunately we still have the time, resources, and intellectual capital to do this—if only we recognize the urgent necessity for change.

From Subprime Blues to Financial Democracy

Although the subject comes up only rarely in the public discourse on the current financial crisis, the advent of subprime mortgages during the 1990s reflected a start, albeit primitive, toward extending the benefits of financial innovation to more and more people—in other words, toward democratizing finance. Prominent commentators, from former Fed chief Alan Greenspan through the late real estate economist Edward Gramlich, considered the subprime mortgage movement a positive development (despite some abusive lending practices) because it effectively expanded the franchise for asset ownership to millions of low-income people.

But subprime mortgages, for all their lofty social aspirations, were a disaster in their implementation: they

23

lacked the kind of risk-management institutions necessary to support the increasingly complex financial machinery needed to underwrite them—the subject of this book.

If safe, effective, and enlightened approaches to designing risk-management institutions can be deployed as the basis for future market activity, the subprime crisis cannot merely be solved—it can be transformed in its aftermath into a better environment for extending the financial franchise, for further democratizing finance.

The first assumption underlying such an effort is the need to better understand the risks inherent in real estate and to acquire the know-how to more efficiently spread these risks. The subprime mortgages, for all their democratic appeal, were launched with a woeful failure to understand real estate risks.

A second assumption is that the democratic extension of the innovations of modern financial technology must be done with a clearer understanding of human psychology, so that the spreading of risk can foster proper economic incentives and limit moral hazard. The subprime crisis was essentially psychological in origin, as are all bubbles. The crisis was not caused by the impact of a meteor or the explosion of a volcano. Rather it was caused by failure to anticipate quite obvious risks—by "irrational exuberance" at the prospects for profits, if one bought into the concept of an ever-expanding bubble.

Ultimately the solution to the economic problems revealed by the subprime crisis requires our doing a much better job of extending the innovations of modern financial technology, together with effective safeguards, throughout society, and of being unafraid to think and act on the scale of the New Deal–era reformers. Democratizing finance is crucial in this process: by spreading risk, it places economic life on a firmer foundation. Financial democracy is thus not only an end in itself, but a means to another, equally worthy, end: the propagation of greater economic stability and prosperity by financial means.

The democratization of finance has in a limited sense already been embodied in the so-called microfinance revolution. The 2006 Nobel Peace Prize, awarded to Muhammad Yunus and the Grameen Bank, has given new impetus to the innovations they set in motion. The microfinance revolution consists of novel institutions that make loans to the tiniest of businesses, often in the least-developed parts of the world.

Yunus has received a sympathetic hearing from world leaders in China, Russia, and elsewhere. More broadly, leaders in emerging countries around the world are showing interest in bringing financial services to more and more people. Mexican president Felipe Calderón has called for policies to promote "financial culture" in his country. The Inter-American Development Bank has launched an action campaign to expand the range of financial services available to the general population throughout Latin America.

Yet another initiative associated with financial democracy is that of the Peruvian policy innovator Hernando de Soto, author of *The Mystery of Capital*, whose work in asserting the importance of property rights in developing countries has underscored the vital link between legal property ownership among the poor and access to financial capital from domestic and foreign sources alike.

Some of the components of the subprime solution outlined in this book are in the same vein as these initiatives, yet there are differences. The measures called for here are, in the first instance, intended for the most advanced countries. They are not only for the poor, but also for people who are struggling to make do with modest incomes, and indeed for everyone. This book is about dealing with the subprime crisis, and future crises like it, by *developing a new financial infrastructure for the entire population,* and doing so using the most advanced technology at our disposal.

A Road Map of This Book

In the remaining chapters of this book I describe the current subprime crisis with an eye toward understanding its dimensions and its psychological origins. Then I detail both short-term and long-term solutions. Central to this brief manifesto will be the need for action. Reforming the institutional framework is an urgent task, to which we must turn immediately if we are to halt the damage caused by the subprime crisis and learn from it, so that we can move forward to a new and better economic system.

Housing in History

The housing bubble was a major cause, if not *the* cause, of the subprime crisis and of the broader economic crisis we now face. The perception that real estate prices could only go up, year after year, established an atmosphere that invited lenders and financial institutions to loosen their standards and risk default. Now the defaults are happening, massively and contagiously.

As of this writing, according to the Standard & Poor's / Case-Shiller Home Price Indices, which I helped create, U.S. home prices have already fallen nearly halfway back down to their pre-bubble levels. The rate of fall of prices has been speeding up.

Nominal price decreases will eventually slow down and stop, but may not then keep up with general inflation. Continuing real price drops could eventually bring us all the way back down from the recent historic peak in places in the United States and other countries as well. The cumulated price declines could severely test our economic institutions. The relatively slight price declines already recorded have thus far produced a crisis of mortgage defaults for relatively few mortgage holders, and the impact to date on the financial institutions that issued, insured, or held these mortgages may be minor compared to the damage that may yet unfold. Many hedge funds are highly leveraged, and further declines in asset values may put those who are, as of now, still looking strong far under water. Their failure would in turn put pressure on banks and other financial institutions.

Or, the problem could express itself in more general inflation, which central banks might tolerate because inflation tends to support nominal home prices and bails out borrowers by reducing the real value of debt. While we may wish to think of the subprime problem as a one-act play, soon to end, it could in fact be but the first act of a long and complex tragedy.

Revealing History

In 2004, when I was writing the second edition of *Irrational Exuberance*—updating and expanding what had been a book largely about the stock market boom of the

1990s to cover the real estate boom of the 2000s as well—I wanted to include an analysis of the long-term performance of the housing market. This would have paralleled the approach I had taken to the stock market in the first edition.

To my surprise, everyone I asked said that there *were* no data on the long-term performance of home prices—not for the United States, nor for any country. Stop and think about that. If the housing boom is such a spectacular economic event, wouldn't you imagine that someone would care if this kind of thing had happened before, and what the outcome had been? But, amazingly, nobody seemed interested in what had happened more than thirty or so years ago. This is at once a lesson in human behavior and a reminder that human attention is capricious. Clearly *no one* was carefully evaluating the real estate market and its potential for speculative excess.

I found that, at various times over the past century or so, economists had indeed constructed price indices of existing homes, but only for relatively short time intervals. Until recent decades, no one had produced these on an ongoing basis. Thus the earlier price indices remained as merely isolated scraps of historical data.

So I constructed my own index of U.S. existing-home prices dating all the way back to 1890. I did so by linking together various available series that seemed to be of the highest quality. I chose only indices that were designed to provide estimates of the price of a standard, unchanging house, so that the price index would represent the outcome of an investment in a house and would not be affected by the general upward trend in the size and quality of homes through time. I could find no index at all for the years 1934–53, and so I had my research assistants fill that gap by tabulating prices in for-sale-by-owner ads in old newspapers. That period remains the weakest link in my index, but I did the best I could do to fill the gap.

Figure 2.1 in the second (2005) edition of *Irrational Exuberance* showed the real (corrected for consumer price inflation) home-price index, along with building costs, the population of the United States, and the long-term interest rate, over the period 1890–2004. The very same figure is shown here, also as Figure 2.1, updated; the continuations of the curves since 2004 are shown in gray rather than black. I wrote in the second edition that home prices were looking *very* anomalous at that time, like a "rocket taking off."* Real home prices for the United States as a whole increased 85% between 1997 and the peak in 2006. Home prices certainly did not seem justifiable in terms of changes in the other variables shown in

*Robert J. Shiller, *Irrational Exuberance,* 2nd Edition (Princeton, N.J.: Princeton University Press), 2005, p. 12.

Figure 2.1.
U.S. Real Home Prices, 1890–2008, along with Building Costs, Population, and Long-Term Government Bond Interest Rates, annual 1890–2008. *Source:* From Robert J. Shiller, *Irrational Exuberance,* 2nd Edition (Princeton, N.J.: Princeton University Press, 2005), p. 13, updated here, with updates shown in gray. Home price index is shown quarterly for 2007-I to 2008-I.

the figure. It looked like the rocket might come crashing back down to earth.

And, as is obvious from the gray segment of the home price curve, the data do indeed show a sharp drop in home prices after 2006. The rocket has fallen—and the bust after the peak was not explainable by any significant change in the other variables.

Ratios of home prices to building costs had soared in the run-up to the peak of the market in 2006, as had ratios of home prices to rent and home prices to personal income. Now these ratios are falling. The misalignment of home prices with economic fundamentals is strongly suggestive of economic instability. And it is evidence of a problem that may not go away until prices correct massively. There are certain basic economic laws that—while they may be bent over short intervals—ultimately always assert themselves in the long run.

Diversity of Price Paths

The seemingly unprecedented behavior of national home prices since the late 1990s is in fact not unprecedented if one looks at individual cities. Housing markets in some cities have gone through spectacular booms in the past. But the fraction of cities experiencing booms has increased dramatically in the recent boom. Figure 2.2 shows examples of some of our major metropolitan areas, again with the S&P/Case-Shiller Home Price Indices corrected for inflation. The figure reveals differences in price behavior across cities. Real estate is still a market where location counts. But despite these differences across cities *before* the peak in 2006, *now* they are *all* declining. The rate of decline is roughly inversely propor-

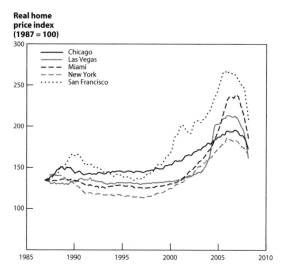

Figure 2.2
Real Home Prices in a Sample of Cities, Monthly, January 1983
to March 2008. *Source:* Author's calculations using data from
www.homeprice.standardandpoors.com and www.bls.gov.

tional to the speed of the increase. As the figure shows,
Las Vegas, Miami, and San Francisco have both risen
faster before 2006 and declined faster afterward than the
more stable cities Chicago and New York.

In addition to differences across metropolitan areas,
there were also differences across segments *within* these
markets. Note that there are separate markets by price
tier: low-priced homes behave considerably differently
through time than high-priced homes. Figure 2.3 shows

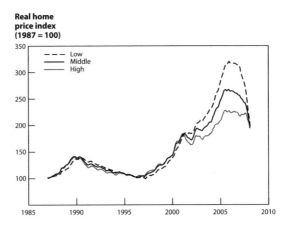

Real home price index (1987 = 100)

- - - Low
——— Middle
········ High

Figure 2.3
Real San Francisco Metro Area Home-Price Indices by Price Tier,
Monthly, January 1987 to March 2008. *Source:* Author's calculations
using data from www.homeprice.standardandpoors.com and
www.bls.gov.

the example of metropolitan San Francisco, broken down
into three price tiers.

The lowest price tier showed the biggest increases
during the recent boom, until 2006, and the biggest drop
afterward. The same phenomenon may be observed in
many cities. What accounts for this difference across tiers
is not known precisely, but a good candidate to explain
it is the subprime phenomenon. The steep increases are
due to the rapid expansion since 2001 of subprime loans,
which were provided in increasing numbers to lower-
income buyers and for the purpose of financing the pur-

chase of lower-priced homes and investor properties. And the more rapid fall in lower-tier home prices since the 2006 peak of the boom appears to be consonant with the problems of default and foreclosure in that tier.

However, even though there have been differences in price behavior across price tiers, we still see that the behavior of all price tiers is basically similar. There was a boom in low-priced homes, in midprice homes, and in high-priced homes, and now the boom is unraveling in all these markets.

While some countries have still-booming housing markets, there are many that show patterns like the United States. Figure 2.4 shows a comparison of real home prices in greater London and greater Boston. The overall similarity between the cities, on opposite sides of the Atlantic, is striking. There are of course differences, but the broad patterns are indeed similar. Both cities experienced booms in the 1980s. Both experienced collapse in the early 1990s. Both cities experienced rapidly rising home prices in the early 2000s. Home prices in both are declining sharply according to the latest data.

The pervasiveness of the boom of the early 2000s across cities, across price tiers, and across countries suggests that something very broad and general has been at work. We cannot explain the bubble in terms of factors specific to any one of these markets. I argue in the next

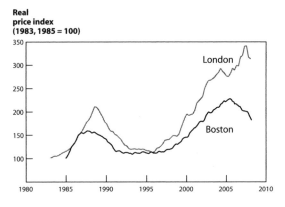

Real price index (1983, 1985 = 100)

Figure 2.4
Real Greater London and Greater Boston Home Prices.
Source: London prices quarterly 1983-I to 2008-I are from the Halifax House Price Index, divided by the U.K. Retail Prices Index. U.S. prices monthly January 1983 to March 2008 are from the S&P/Case-Shiller Home Price Indices, divided by the Consumer Price Index.

chapter that an important ultimate cause of these extraordinary price movements in so many different places is related to the contagion of market psychology—a contagion that knew no borders because of the global nature of the story that fed it.

Bubble Trouble

Let us look again at Figure 2.1, which shows home prices since 1890. What in the world has been happening since the late 1990s to propel home prices up so dramatically?

The figure shows that there were no fundamental changes in construction costs, population, or long-term interest rates at the time of the boom. So what *was* the cause?

Whatever it was, it was not seen by national leaders, especially not in the United States, where pride in the superiority of our capitalist system sometimes seems to approach religious fervor. During this housing boom, most of our authorities simply denied there was a problem. Alan Greenspan, in his 2007 book *The Age of Turbulence,* recalled what he used to say about the housing boom: "I would tell audiences that we were facing not a bubble but a froth—lots of small local bubbles that never grew to a scale that could threaten the health of the overall economy."[*]

President Bush virtually never mentioned the housing boom in his public pronouncements while it was happening. He referred only to successes. In one of his weekly radio addresses to the nation, in 2005, he boasted that "mortgage rates are low. And over the past year the home-ownership rate in America has reached record levels."[†]

Ben Bernanke, then chairman of the President's Council of Economic Advisers, said in 2005: "House prices have risen by nearly 25 percent over the past two years. Although speculative activity has increased in some areas, at a national level these price increases largely reflect strong economic fundamentals, including robust growth in jobs and incomes, low mortgage rates, steady rates of household formation, and factors that limit the expansion of housing supply in some areas."[‡]

These people were certainly aware of the possibility of bubbles. Indeed Greenspan must have been thinking of this when I and my colleague John Y. Campbell, along with others, were asked to testify before the Fed-

---

[*] Alan Greenspan, *The Age of Turbulence: Adventures in a New World* (New York: Penguin, 2007), p. 231.

[†] George W. Bush, "President's Radio Address," August 6, 2005, http://www.whitehouse.gov/news/releases/2005/08/20050806.html.

[‡] Ben S. Bernanke, "The Economic Outlook," October 20, 2005, http://www.whitehouse.gov/cea/econ-outlook20051020.html.

eral Reserve Board on December 3, 1996, two days before Greenspan made his famous "irrational exuberance" speech. He heard us out. His autobiography reveals that he was wrestling with the idea of bubbles. But he concluded, as did so many others, that bubbles were not tangible enough to justify any policy changes.

Something was going on—in both the stock market bubble of the 1990s and the real estate bubble that followed it—that these leaders found very difficult to see as it was happening. So it will necessarily be something of a challenge for us to understand what it was.

A Contagion of Ideas

While every historical event is the outcome of a combination of factors, I believe, as I argued in *Irrational Exuberance,* that the most important single element to be reckoned with in understanding this or any other speculative boom is the *social contagion* of boom thinking, mediated by the common observation of rapidly rising prices. This social contagion lends increasing credibility to stories—I call them "new era" stories—that appear to justify the belief that the boom will continue. The operation of such a social contagion of ideas is hard to see because we do not observe the contagion directly, and it is easy to neglect its underlying causes.

Some observers seem to be ideologically opposed to the idea that contagion of thought patterns plays any role in our collective thinking. Indeed, people think the world is led by independent minds who invariably act with great intelligence. Since the bubble years of the late 1990s, intellectual arrogance of this kind appears to have exerted a growing influence over the world economy.

Alan Greenspan, in a *Financial Times* op-ed piece in March 2008, recognized—well after the bubble was over—that there had indeed been "euphoria" and "speculative fever." But, he wrote, "The essential problem is that our models—both risk models and econometric models—as complex as they have become—are still too simple to capture the full array of governing variables that drive global economic reality. A model, of necessity, is an abstraction from the full detail of the real world."*

Greenspan thus did eventually acknowledge the obvious reality of bubbles, but he never seemed to embrace the view that a good part of what drives people's thinking is purely social in nature. He espoused the idea that the mathematical econometric models of individual behavior are the only tools that we will ever have with which to understand the world, and that they are limited only by the amount and nature of our data and our ability to deal

---

*Alan Greenspan, "We Will Never Have a Perfect Model of Risk," *Financial Times,* March 17, 2008, p. 9.

with complexity. He does not seem to respect research approaches from the fields of psychology or sociology.

Perhaps his lack of attention to bubbles reflected, at least in part, an overly strong ideological alignment with some of the views of his former mentor, the philosopher Ayn Rand. She idealized the strength of individual, independent, courageous action and rational selfish man as a "heroic being." But a tendency to base one's self-esteem on a belief in the possibility of economic success through individual action goes far beyond the admirers of Ayn Rand.

What seems to be absent from the thinking of many economists and economic commentators is an understanding that contagion of ideas is consistently a factor in human affairs. Just as there are interregional differences in matters of opinion (as evidenced, for example, by the geographic concentration of support for political parties), so too are there intertemporal differences. The changing zeitgeist drives common opinion among the members of society at any point in time and place, and this zeitgeist changes as new ideas gain prominence and recede in importance within the collective thinking. Speculative markets are merely exceptionally good places in which to observe the ebb and flow of the zeitgeist.

Understanding such a social contagion is a lot like understanding a disease epidemic. Epidemics crop up from time to time, and their timing often baffles experts. But a mathematical theory of epidemiology has been developed, and it can help medical authorities better understand these apparently mysterious events.

Every disease has a contagion rate (the rate at which it is spread from person to person) and a removal rate (the rate at which individuals recover from or succumb to the illness and so are no longer contagious). If the contagion rate exceeds the removal rate by a necessary amount, an epidemic begins. The contagion rate varies through time because of a number of factors. For example, contagion rates for influenza are higher in the winter, when lower temperatures encourage the spread of the virus in airborne droplets after infected individuals sneeze.

So it is in the economic and social environment. Sooner or later, some factor boosts the infection rate sufficiently above the removal rate for an optimistic view of the market to become widespread. There is an escalation in public knowledge of the arguments that would seem to support that view, and soon the epidemic spirals up and out of control. Almost everyone appears to think—if they notice at all that certain economic arguments are more in evidence—that the arguments are increasingly heard only because of their true intellectual merit. The idea that the prominence of the arguments is in fact due to a social contagion is hardly ever broached, at least not outside university sociology departments.

In the recent speculative housing boom, an optimistic view of the market was certainly much in evidence. In a survey that Karl Case and I conducted in 2005, when the market was booming, we found that the median expected price increase among San Francisco home buyers over the next ten years was 9% a year, and the mean expected price increase was 14% a year. About a third of the respondents reported truly extravagant expectations—occasionally over 50% a year. On what did they base such outlooks? They had observed significant price increases and heard others' interpretation of such increases. We were witnessing the contagion of an interpretation or a way of forming expectations.

An important part of what happens during a speculative bubble is mediated by the marketplace, to which many people are attentive, and by the prices that are observed there and subsequently amplified by the news media. What do we mean by "amplified" in this context? The media weave stories around price movements, and when those movements are upward, the media tend to embellish and legitimize "new era" stories with extra attention and detail. Feedback loops appear, as price increases encourage belief in "new era" stories, promote the contagion of those stories, and so lead to further price increases. The price–story–price loop repeats again and again during a speculative bubble.

The feedback loops also take the form of price–economic activity–price loops. Speculative price increases encourage genuine economic optimism, hence more spending, hence greater economic growth, hence yet more optimism, hence further bidding up of prices. Most persons can be forgiven for not seeing that the sense of economic prosperity that usually attends a major speculative bubble is actually caused by the bubble itself and not by economic fundamentals.

Under certain circumstances the explanations for contagion and feedback during speculative bubbles may be perfectly rational, and "rational bubbles" can be part of the story. A number of economic theorists have discussed the possibility of such bubbles.

The essential element of these rational bubble theories is that people may learn about the information that others have by observing their behavior. They cannot respond directly to the information that others have, since they cannot see inside their heads. But they may base their own decisions on the *actions* of others (as when they bid up speculative prices), which they interpret, wholly rationally, as reflecting valid information about economic fundamentals.

The problem is that we can arrive at a situation in which people are generally adopting an excessively optimistic (or excessively pessimistic) view, because they are rationally but mistakenly judging the information that others have. To borrow a term used by economic theorists Sushil Bikhchandani, David Hirshleifer, and Ivo Welch, speculative bubbles may be caused by "information cascades." An information cascade occurs when those in a group disregard their own independent, individually collected information (which might otherwise encourage them *not* to subscribe to a boom or other mass belief) because they feel that everyone else simply couldn't be wrong. And when they disregard their own independent information, and act instead on general information as they perceive it, they squelch their own information. It is no longer available to the group and so does not figure in further collective judgments. Thus, over time, the quality of group information declines.

Psychological, epidemiological, and economic theory all point to an environment in which feedback of enthusiasm for speculative assets, or feedback of price increases into further price increases, can be expected to produce speculative bubbles from time to time. They make clear that these bubbles can have complicated—sometimes random and unpredictable—dynamics.

Other "Causes" of the Bubble

The interpretation of the bubble that I have just offered is not the conventional wisdom. Other factors are widely cited as the cause of the housing boom. I argue here that, to a large extent, these other factors were themselves substantially a *product* of the bubble, and not exogenous factors that caused the bubble.

The U.S. Federal Reserve cut its key rate, the federal funds rate, to 1% in mid-2003 and held it there until mid-2004, roughly the period of most rapid home-price increase. Moreover, the real (inflation-corrected) federal funds rate was negative for thirty-one months, from October 2002 to April 2005, an interval again centered on the most rapid rise in home prices. Since 1950 the only other period of low rates as long as this one was the thirty-seven-month interval from September 1974 to September 1977.

We should not, however, view this period of very loose monetary policy as an *exogenous* cause of the bubble. For the monetary policy—both that of the Fed and that of other central banks around the world—was driven by economic conditions that were created by the bursting of the stock market bubble of the 1990s, and the real estate boom was itself in some ways a repercussion of that same stock market bubble.

This loose policy would not have been implemented if Alan Greenspan and others involved with monetary policy had comprehended that we were going through a housing bubble that would burst. Thus the monetary policy appears to have been driven at least in part by the same lack of understanding that produced the bubble itself. The Fed was excessively focused on preventing recession and deflation because they honestly saw the home-price increases as continuing—if at a reduced pace—indefinitely, even if they were to implement a monetary policy that would feed the bubble.

The interest rate cuts cannot explain the general nine-year upward trend that we have seen in the housing market. The housing boom period was three times as long as the period of low interest rates, and the housing boom was accelerating when the Fed was increasing interest rates in 1999. Moreover, long-term interest rates, which determine the rates for fixed-rate conventional mortgages, did not respond in any substantial way to these rate cuts until the late stages of the boom.

The impact of the loose monetary policy was amplified by the large number of adjustable-rate mortgages issued after 2000, particularly to subprime borrowers. These mortgages were more responsive than fixed-rate mortgages to the cuts that the Fed had made. So the rate cuts might have had the effect of boosting the boom, more than would otherwise have been the case, during its time of most rapid ascent, around 2004.

Adjustable-rate mortgages were common because those who had been influenced by bubble thinking and wanted to get into real estate investments as heavily as possible were demanding them. The mere fact that interest payments would be going up soon did not deter them. They expected to be compensated by rapidly increasing home prices, and they believed that those higher prices would permit them to refinance at a lower rate. Subprime borrowers wanted these mortgages in disproportionate numbers both because they were less quantitatively sophisticated and because they were consumed by the mere thought of somehow gaining a foothold in the housing market.

The demand for loans made with more flexible standards was accommodated by lenders because they themselves (as well as the investors in the mortgages that they sold off) believed in the bubble. That is why the period of soaring real estate prices corresponded to a time when no-documentation loans became common and when option ARMs and other questionable new mortgage types proliferated.

Moreover, the rating agencies that pass judgment on securitized mortgages persisted in giving AAA ratings to mortgage securities that ultimately were vulnerable because they too believed that there would be no bursting of the bubble. Even if they did harbor some doubts about the continuation of the boom, they were not about to take the drastic step of cutting ratings on securitized mortgage products on the basis of the *theory,* not widely held, that home prices *might* actually fall. That would have been an unusually courageous step—and one that was all too easily postponed in favor of other business decisions that were easier to make, until it was too late.

Another factor often mentioned as a cause of the housing bubble is the failure of regulators to rein in aggressive lending. Ever since the Depository Institutions Deregulatory and Monetary Control Act of 1980 effectively ended state usury laws, and made it possible for originators to make a profit with subprime lending by charging a high enough interest rate to offset the costs of the inevitable defaults and foreclosures, there had been a need for expanding the scope of regulation. Yet the expanded regulation never came, and over time during the 1990s and into the 2000s, a "shadow banking system" of nonbank mortgage originators was allowed to develop without anything like the regulation to which banks are subject.

But the lack of urgency among regulators in doing their job must ultimately have originated in their inability to believe that there could ever be a housing crisis of the proportions we are seeing today.

When I gave talks near the peak of the bubble in 2005 at the Office of the Comptroller of the Currency and the Federal Deposit Insurance Corporation, both major bank regulators in the United States, I found staff members there in disagreement about what to do about the lending boom. I urged them to take prompt action to stop the excess of mortgage lending that was feeding an unsustainable bubble. The reaction I got was that, yes, they understood that *maybe* they should, and that indeed *some* among them thought so, but that it was just taking time—and negotiation—to arrive at any strong consensus. I had the feeling that many of them viewed me, with my argument that the bubble would burst, as an extremist who deserved a skeptical response.

When in October 2006 I participated in a panel sponsored by the Yale Investment Club, I shared the dais with Frank Nothaft, chief economist at Freddie Mac, a major securitizer of home mortgages. As I recall the event now, I asked him if Freddie Mac had stress-tested the impact on itself of a possible housing price decline. He answered that they had, and they had even considered the possibility of a 13.4% national drop in home prices. I protested: "What about the possibility of a drop that is bigger than that?" He answered that such a drop had never happened, at least not since the Great Depression.

During the housing market debacle after the 1980s home-price boom, the U.S. government passed the Federal Housing Enterprises Financial Safety and Soundness Act of 1992 (GSE Act), which in turn created the Office of Federal Housing Enterprise Oversight (OFHEO) to oversee the risks to government-sponsored enterprises Fannie Mae and Freddie Mac. One of OFHEO's objectives, specified in the act, was to prevent even the possibility of a financial freeze-up. OFHEO is still with us today, watching out for possible systemic risks. The GSE Act required that OFHEO develop a stress test that simulates possible adverse interest rate and credit risk scenarios, and OFHEO has done so.

However, in its annual reports to Congress through 2007, OFHEO never showed any recognition of the housing boom that has been the main cause of the risks, let alone any understanding of its psychological origins. These regulators did not seem to see the risk, and they allowed Freddie and Fannie to go on supporting the housing boom.

Ultimately an important reason why all these factors fed the bubble has to be that the very people responsible for oversight were caught up in the same high expectations for future home-price increases that the general public had. In many cases they may not have believed as zealously in the housing boom, but they nevertheless accepted the received wisdom that it could not end badly. And that was the end of the story.

Evidence that institutions never expected these costly defaults can be seen in the total disarray in which many found themselves as the subprime market melted down. For example, by the end of 2007 banks were begging to be relieved from the requirements of Financial Accounting Standard 114. This rule, issued by the Financial Accounting Standards Board, requires banks to report bad loans (so-called impaired loans) based on the present value of future cash flows. It is an attempt to standardize the reporting of such liabilities and thus make it harder to conceal them in regulatory filings. The banks protested that they had never developed the computing power to handle the volume of such loan restructuring. They didn't develop it because they absolutely did not see the crisis coming.

This disarray is shown most clearly in the financial freeze-up that we have been experiencing around the world. Businesses of all varieties, in many countries, left their balance sheets vulnerable to changes in the prices of assets that were—directly or indirectly—tied to the real estate market.

The weakening of credit standards that led to this situation is part of the normal process of a speculative bubble, as was argued long ago by economists Hyman Minsky and Charles Kindleberger. In a climate of excessive optimism, people tend to take full advantage of a strong economy instead of protecting themselves from the possibility of a major correction—an eventuality that seems to them utterly remote.

Changes in the Thinking That Creates Bubbles

So the new belief that investing in homes was just an awfully good idea fed the bubble after the late 1990s. But, one wonders, why did this happen just then? Why had such thinking not caught on, nationally or internationally, before? What made bubble thinking especially contagious after 2000?

It is not as if people were not interested in speculation before 2000. Hardly. In fact, land speculation was a widespread and well-known phenomenon, going far back into history.

In his 1932 book *The Great American Land Bubble: The Amazing Story of Land-Grabbing, Speculations, and Booms from Colonial Days to the Present Time,* the historian Aaron Sakolski argued that an atmosphere of speculation dates back to the beginnings of U.S. history. The opening line of the book says it all: "America, from its inception, was a speculation."* It was widely perceived

---

*Aaron Sakolski, *The Great American Land Bubble: The Amazing Story of Land-Grabbing, Speculations, and Booms from Colonial Days to the Present Time* (New York: Harper and Brothers, 1932), p. 1.

by the eighteenth century, Sakolski argued, that America would eventually be populated much more densely by vast numbers of immigrants. Land speculators from the late 1600s onward would buy thousands of acres for a shilling an acre and hope to sell them many years later to immigrants, doubling or tripling their money. There were waves of speculative mania, and land apparently sometimes became overpriced, leading to drops and to the ruination of speculators. Indeed the fever for land speculation infected some in the highest places. No less an early American than George Washington, according to Sakolski, was a land speculator.

Homer Hoyt, in his 1933 book *One Hundred Years of Land Values in Chicago,* paints a similar picture of speculation in land values in the city of Chicago, which, he said, came to an end in the late 1920s because "the speculative public was forsaking real estate for the stock market."* But, like Sakolski, Hoyt was talking mostly about *land* speculation (in choice lots and blocks within the Chicago metropolitan area), not about individual homeowners buying homes in ordinary neighborhoods in the hope of making a profit.

It is not coincidental, by the way, that both of these classic accounts of real estate speculation appeared right

---

*Homer Hoyt, *One Hundred Years of Land Values in Chicago* (Chicago: University of Chicago Libraries, 1933), p. 265.

at the peak of the last great real estate crisis in the 1930s. That was when the public was most interested in real estate speculation. We have entered another era of heightened attention to real estate speculation, and new books about housing speculation have been appearing in great numbers. The focus on the real estate market that has increased the social contagion of bubble thinking appears to be related to the aftereffects of the stock market boom of the 1990s.

That boom involved a transformation of people's thinking about their role in the economy. The idea developed that we ought to expect to make a lot of money investing. The transformation went well beyond opinions about particular investment strategies to alter the very self-esteem mechanism that supports our egos. The Protestant work ethic that had underlain the national psyche for so long underwent a makeover. To a substantial extent, we no longer admired those who were merely hard workers. To be truly revered, one had to be a smart investor as well.

It is the change in thinking about ourselves that is the deepest cause of the bubble, and may be slowest to unravel after the bubble comes to an end. George Akerlof and Rachel Kranton have shown persuasively that economic theorists must take as fundamental that people care more about who they are and how they are viewed than the kind of food they are eating or car they are driving.* A life as an investor has become more than a means to an end, it is an end in itself.

Since the 1990s we have also come increasingly to think that the movers and shakers of the world are smart investors too. We began to believe that nascent capitalism in China, India, Russia, Brazil, and other less-advanced countries was producing a vast new class of the wealthy, who would bid up the price of real estate and other assets that were in limited supply. Of course these countries really *were* developing. The mistake was in exaggerating the significance of these stories of emerging capitalism for the real estate market of today.

What is different with the recent bubble, in comparison with earlier bubbles, is that the "new era" story is one of economic pressures that will raise the price of every available piece of real estate. Real estate bubbles from other times in history have always been relatively local, and the story that was seen to explain the bubble did not generalize to cover real estate everywhere.

The Florida land bubble that peaked in 1925, the biggest real estate bubble during the first half of the twentieth century, apparently spread a good deal beyond Florida, but it nevertheless had a relatively modest effect on urban home prices nationwide. National real home

*George Akerlof and Rachel Kranton, "The Economics of Identity," *Quarterly Journal of Economics*, 115(3):715–753, 2000.

prices increased only 19% between 1921 and the peak of the bubble in 1925. The story then was essentially that Florida was being discovered, as the automobile proliferated, as an accessible place, and that land there was running out. That story would never be seen as justifying a boom in Cincinnati or Toronto.

Local housing booms certainly occurred long ago. There were housing booms even in the legendary days when the cowboys and Indians still roamed the American West. How could there have been a housing boom *then*, when the American West was still very much a frontier and land was extraordinarily abundant? But there was—in southern California, when people from all over the country converged there to speculate in homes. And, yes, there was a story then about California that justified the bubble, once again a story that did not generalize to other states.

The California bubble built up in the 1880s, peaked in 1887, and burst in 1888. Newspapers around the United States wrote abundantly about it as it happened, and the articles repeatedly praised the wonderful climate, beautiful scenery, and California lifestyle.

On the other hand there was also a great deal of contemporary skepticism as to why the California boom had assumed the proportions it did. A story in the *Los Angeles Times* of December 26, 1887, entitled "The Southern

Boom," recounted the observations of one reporter from out of town:

> At Los Angeles, the true home of the boom, you arrive at the hotel and are told they can give you meals but no bed. You scowl, scratch your head, and wish that every fool had not come to town the same day that you did. You sally forth, and at last are given a cot in the hall, and you are happy.
>
> In the morning you start out to see the sights, and you begin to see them within the first block you go, and the further on you travel the more you see. You are continually inclined to paraphrase the old song "Mine eyes have seen the glory of the lord" with "Mine eyes have seen the marvel of the boom." But they have not. You can travel around for days in Los Angeles and not see it all. It is useless to attempt to describe it. As well try to count the stars in Heaven as to number the new buildings in construction at the present time. . . .
>
> "What has done all this?" you ask. We answer: "The boom." "Well, what is the boom?" you inquire. We made the same inquiry of dozens of men in all avocations of life, and none could give us an answer. We were told it is something unprecedented in the financial and economic experience of the country. We

asked if it would last, and were told that as it came unbidden, it would probably be as erratic in its going.*

The talk reported in this article is much the same as that we heard in the 2000s, with the same amazement about the price surge and the resulting construction activity, the same puzzlement about why it was happening.

Judging from newspaper stories written around the United States during the boom of the 1880s, the boom was national in the sense that everyone around the country had heard of it, and many from other states were rushing to southern California to participate in it. But there was no suggestion that it was national in the sense that people thought it would infect *their* city. For the story accompanying this boom always stressed that this was a California boom, and that it was driven by the appreciation of the rare beauty and climate of that area.

Still there are puzzles. California is a vast area, and the wonderful climate covers much of this area, and there was abundant farmland and raw land in the 1880s on which new homes could be built. But it must have seemed somehow plausible to many that the cities of California were shaping up to be such unique and desirable places that homes there were uniquely valuable and would stay that way.

---

*"The Southern Boom," *Los Angeles Times*, December 26, 1887, p. 6.

How else could they justify paying high prices for a home in the 1880s in a California city when they could buy a huge farm just a short distance away? In a way, of course, they were right: Los Angeles today remains very important—a hub of social, cultural, and economic activity. The error in thinking then was one of proportion—of thinking that prices there would rise so much and so fast from the 1880s going forward.

Most people do not understand the true nature of the bubble and try to think of speculative events as rational responses to information, for they do not understand contagion of thought. Their thinking tends to accept as simple fact the stories that accompany the bubble.

Understanding Public Thinking during Bubbles

What has changed since the 1990s to make us suddenly avid speculators in homes in so many different places? Trying to answer that question requires that we go back to consider the forces that generate bubbles. Why, for example, was there a tulip mania in Holland in the 1630s— and why has the speculative fascination with tulips since left our collective consciousness?

I discussed this subject at some length in *Irrational Exuberance*, especially its second edition, and I present only some basic ideas here. There is something about the current collection of easily recalled views and ideas that encourages bubble thinking about homes, and, apparently, as well about oil prices and grain prices, though it is hard to pin down.

The new era story about the emergence of capitalist institutions over much of the world—notably emerging countries like China and India—has captured the imagination of speculators, and their imagination connects this story with prices in many different markets, including energy, grains, even gold and other metals. The exaggerated attention to this story is behind the world energy crisis and the world food crisis as well as the housing bubble.

Most analysts do not see the link between all these speculative events. For example, some analysts—notably Paul Krugman—have claimed that there can be no bubble in oil prices because oil stockpiles have not soared, implying that speculators are not actively affecting the demand for oil.* But, despite the evidence from the stockpiles, the price of oil is, just as the price of housing, inherently and deeply speculative. The popular opinion that oil prices will be very high or even higher far into the future—as evidenced by oil futures prices—reduces incentives for producers to invest aggressively today in new extraction facilities, or for regulators to allow the

*Paul Krugman, "The Oil Nonbubble," *New York Times*, May 12, 2008, A19.

environmental impact of rapid exploitation of oil sands, drilling oil offshore, or building new pipelines. The speculative stores of oil are mostly in the ground, and people are happy to leave them there for now despite high prices because they think prices may go higher, not lower.

The new era story we have been experiencing during this massive housing bubble somehow conflates land values with housing values. This admixture is in part simply the result of the bubble itself. It used to be that the underlying land typically constituted only 15% or so of the value of a home in a typical city. So people thought of their homes as depreciating manufactured goods, like cars and boats, which require a lot of upkeep and eventually go out of style. But now that land value (defined as the price of a home minus the estimated cost of building the structure) is often over 50% of home value, we are starting to think of houses as if they are land. Since we see homes every day, there is a naturally high contagion rate, during a new bubble, for a story that describes homes as the best investment one can make.

The error that we are making is to think of this situation of heightened land values as a new equilibrium. There will be a natural process of finding ways to build homes on less land, or less expensive land. This can be achieved either through building higher-density housing, such as more and taller apartment buildings or infill development in urban centers, or founding new urban areas. But such considerations are three steps ahead of the average home buyer's thinking.

In fact there is plenty of cheap land available. The new thinking is that the land in cities is somehow very different from land elsewhere, that we cannot substitute cheaper land for expensive urban land, even in the long run, and that that will justify the very high expectations for its future price. This is such an important part of our bubble thinking that the next chapter will consider it at length.

The Forecastability of Housing Prices

To understand the recent home-price bubble, it is necessary to reflect on the amazingly high level of forecastability of home prices. The housing market is totally different from the stock market, where prices more nearly resemble a "random walk." In the stock market, prices may go up one day and down the next, with relatively little apparent pattern. But, with housing, the market seemed to go in the same direction year after year. U.S. home prices increased every year from 1997 to 2006. The rate of increase of home prices, which was negative in 1991, increased at a generally increasing rate in most years until 2005—a fourteen-year run of mostly increasing rates of increase of home prices.

Bubble thinking means thinking that the trend in prices will continue. Such thinking is mostly irrational for the stock market, since price trends are usually not consistent there. But, oddly, it seems quite rational for the housing market, at least when it is at the height of a boom. Looking at any of the figures in the last chapter, one is struck by how easy it has often been to forecast the housing market in recent decades.

Karl Case and I first confirmed this forecastability of home prices in an article we wrote for the *American Economic Review* in 1989. The real innovation in that article was our repeat-sales home-price index, which showed for the first time how home prices have actually been behaving. My former student Allan Weiss wanted to put this index into practice, and so in 1991 we set up a company, Case Shiller Weiss Inc., which he headed, to produce the indices. We sold the company in 2002 to Fiserv Inc., where Linda Ladner and David Stiff produce the indices for an S&P index committee under the direction of David Blitzer.

The home-price index that was most talked about in 1991 when we founded our company, the simple median of home prices published by the National Association of Realtors, was very noisy because there were rapid changes in the mix of sales from month to month. Large or high-quality houses may sell in one month, small or low-quality houses in another, and so the series *looked* noisy, just like the stock market. But when Case and I cleared out the noise by basing our index only on changes in prices of individual homes, thereby eliminating this mix problem, we found that home prices move exceptionally smoothly through time.

How can prices be so forecastable? Isn't it supposed to be very hard to forecast speculative prices, and aren't such prices supposed to at least approximate a random walk? Yet our statistical analysis confirmed that home prices *are* quite forecastable.

But how can this be? Isn't this the proverbial "money left on the table" that, according to economic theory, just should not happen? Couldn't somebody make a lot of money simply buying and leveraging property in a housing boom and selling a year or so later? How can it have been so easy to make money in real estate?

The answer is, in fact it *was* easy to make money in real estate during the boom in the 2000s—if one understood the momentum in home prices. Apparently, with better home-price data being published in the 1990s, some smart-money investors decided to take a flyer on this booming market, and those who did it and got out in time generally did succeed. It shouldn't have been that hard to get out in time, either. We had two years of warning of a slowdown before prices actually started dropping.

This apparent profit opportunity was an important cause of the bubble, in that it sustained the feedback that generated the bubble. Indeed people were thinking that they could make a lot of money by buying housing, since they had seen others do it, year after year.

Then why did so many get caught by the bubble? They stopped seeing the bubble as a case of simple momentum that one could ride for a while but that must be exited before the market reversed course. Instead they came to believe the story that the boom would *never* end, as we shall see in the next chapter.

The Real Estate Myth

The recent bubble has greatly encouraged public belief in a long-standing myth—the myth that, because of population growth and economic growth, and with limited land resources available, the price of real estate must inevitably trend strongly upward through time.

Since the late 1990s people have increasingly come to believe in our existing cities—in their uniqueness, in their special status. As we saw in Chapter 3, the strength of this belief seems to be associated more with the idea that the increasingly capitalist world is growing rapidly richer than with the observation that simple population growth is at work in producing higher prices.

Indeed the GDP of advanced countries has been increasing at about 3% a year for many decades, and it stands a good chance of continuing to do so over the long run. The rate of GDP growth is even higher in less-developed countries. This might suggest to some that real home prices should rise at a similar rate. In fact that is not what has been happening, and it is not likely to happen in the future.

The fraction of incomes that is spent on housing in the national income accounts has been fairly constant over the decades—but the rising incomes are expressed not in rising home *prices* but in increasing *amounts* of housing consumed.

If one looks squarely at the issue, it is clear that the rise in value of existing urban areas has shown no tendency at all to make investors rich. If the real prices of homes had risen at just 3% a year over the past century, then we could generally not afford houses that are any better or bigger today than we could then. But we know that homes have in fact gotten much larger and better.

According to the U.S. Census, the average floor area in new one-family houses rose from 1,525 square feet in 1973 to 2,248 square feet in 2006, almost a 50% increase. And floor space is only one measure of home quality.

One can compare the average price of a new home with the Constant Quality Index of Home Prices, computed by the U.S. Census Bureau since the 1960s. The average nominal price of a new home rose by a factor of 8.605 in the thirty-five years between 1963 and 1998.

(I chose a time period ending before the recent bubble, to avoid distortions.) But the Constant Quality Index of New Home Prices, also computed by the Census Bureau, rose by a factor of only 5.928. The ratio of those two factors is 1.452, which could be interpreted to mean that new homes were 45% better overall in 1998 than they were in 1963. By this measure, then, the rate of growth in new home quality was 1.1% a year. This is a good fraction of the growth of real per capita income over that interval, which was 2.4% a year. Moreover, average household size fell from 3.29 persons in the 1960 census to 2.63 persons in the 1990 census, a decline of 0.7% a year. We were able to spend our increased incomes on bigger homes and in spreading out among more homes. And we still had money left over to improve our standard of living in other ways, such as traveling more, spending more on entertainment, and demanding better health care. It is very clear that we were not struggling with relentless increases in home prices that even kept pace with our income.

Construction of New Homes—Outside the Glamour Cities

The economist William Baumol has posited what has come to be known as *Baumol's law*: the costs of those goods or services whose production is amenable to technological progress will tend to decline over time relative to the costs of goods or services that are by their nature not so amenable to technological progress. Thus, for example, the cost of education (which relies on traditional class-room teaching, not something that is heavily benefited by technological progress) will tend to increase over time relative to the cost of manufactured goods (whose production can be improved with new tools, methods, and materials). Baumol's law therefore suggests that the price of homes (at least the structure component of home prices) should fall over time.

Yet the actual building costs for which we have records do not show such a downward trend over the whole century plotted in Figure 2.1, although they did from 1900 to the Depression of the 1930s and over the past twenty years. Clearly, at least the spirit of Baumol's law is being followed: home prices have not shown a strong or consistent upward trend before the bubble that started in the 1990s.

Of course land cannot be built; except for a few artificial islands in Dubai and some other suitable places, the quantity of land is fixed forever. But land is just one input into the production of homes, and if higher land prices in urban areas are pushing up home prices, then there is an incentive for builders to find alternatives to heavy use of this scarce resource.

They can build more densely in urban areas. While there are political forces arguing against increased density (notably the owners of existing homes, who see such construction as a threat to their home values), it is hard to believe that those forces can win out in the long run, given the moral argument for supplying people with homes and the persistence of developers in pursuing opportunities to ply their craft.

And there is a great deal of land to expand to. According to the U.S. Census for the year 2000, urban land area accounts for only 2.6% of total land area in the United States. The high value of homes in major cities is accounted for by their location relative to the built environment, not the unique value of the land. That kind of environment can be reproduced by planned and coordinated efforts.

Urban Patriotism and Parochialism

The belief in so-called glamour cities as loci for fantastic real estate investments has a tinge of patriotic feeling behind it. Many seem to consider their own city as possessing an illusory greatness, to an unhealthy extent.

I had the pleasure of giving an outdoor lunchtime talk to an international group of investment professionals at the beautiful seaside resort of Ozdere, near Izmir,

Turkey. In these pristine surroundings, with a spectacular view over the Aegean Sea to the Greek island of Samos, where the mathematician Pythagoras and the astronomer Aristarchus once lived, I told them about the incredible loyalty that people often show to their own homelands. For example, I told them of Californians' feelings about their home state. I explained that they are very proud of their pleasant weather and beautiful scenery. Californians often say "everyone wants to live here." I know they say that in great numbers, because they write it with some regularity on questionnaires I have sent out asking the recipients to comment on the real estate situation in their home states.

I asked the assembled group in Turkey for a show of hands: "Would you really rather be in California?" No one raised a hand. Probably many of these individuals in Turkey have little knowledge of all the beautiful places in California, just as Californians have little knowledge of all the beautiful places in Turkey. The belief that we are constantly being watched (psychologist Thomas Gilovich calls it the spotlight effect) encourages thoughts that one's own city is more desired than it is.

Loyalty to one's city or state may sound like a good thing, and perhaps that is what programs to promote homeownership are supposed to foster. But it also produces speculative bubbles, and California has been the bubbliest state in the United States.

The solution to this problem is to open up the real estate marketplace to the hard glare of market discipline. We must democratize our markets, as I shall discuss in Chapter 6. Turks—indeed people from all over the world—will be more than happy to sell California real estate short during the next bubble, once markets are liquid enough that they can do so. And that will help prevent mispricings such as those that contributed to the subprime crisis. Such an open market won't prevent all bubbles, of course, but it will most likely enable a system of checks and balances that would prevent a repetition of the extraordinary run-up of home prices, and attendant phenomena in the credit markets, that we have seen recently.

Construction Costs: Myth and Reality

There has been a lot of casual talk during the bubble about "exploding construction costs" in much the same way as there has been talk about running out of land. This talk has fed the impression that we may be running out of building materials, and that this scarcity will make homes much more expensive in the future.

The building cost index that appears in Figure 2.1 does not confirm this scenario, although some other cost measures did show jumps during the bubble, probably reflecting construction bottlenecks. For example, during a housing boom there tends to be a shortage of skilled construction workers, until we eventually train more of them. But the real time period for judging home prices is the long run. Are we really running out of building materials?

The main materials from which dwellings are made today are lumber, plaster, concrete, glass, and steel. How close is the world to running out of these?

Lumber is a renewable resource; it cannot be exhausted. Our principal commercial forests are managed on a continuing basis. Population pressures have not been high in lumber-producing regions. Technical progress has been making the use of lumber more efficient, relying on optimal harvesting rather than clear-cutting, computerized sawmills that reduce waste, improved types of particleboard, and other innovations. Indeed global warming is considered likely, if anything, to *increase* the supply of lumber. Genetic engineering may improve the growth rate of trees.

Gypsum, the main ingredient of plaster and wallboard, is a very common mineral. The White Sands National Monument in New Mexico, famed for its views of massive white gypsum-sand dunes as far as the eye can see, contains 275 square miles of nearly pure gypsum sand. Although this particular site is protected, it is worth noting that White Sands alone would be enough to supply the world's construction industry for hundreds of years.

Limestone, the principal ingredient of the cement used for concrete, represents approximately 10% of all sedimentary rock formations on earth.

Glass is made primarily, and sometimes entirely, from quartz. Quartz is the second most common mineral in the earth's crust.

Iron, the major ingredient of steel, is the fourth most abundant element on the earth's surface, constituting 5% of the surface. It is true that hematite, a popular ore, has been largely depleted in many countries, and fears of running out of iron were expressed there, especially during the two world wars. But there are many other sources and types of ores. Additional iron can come from the recycling of motor vehicles, bridges, the structural components of large buildings, ships, and other scrap materials.

Any of these building materials, should there be a shortage, could be replaced with others. We can build homes without significant amounts of lumber or plaster, or without concrete, or without steel, or even without glass.

In the history of housing, many materials have been used to build homes, including mud, sod, straw, bamboo, paper, snow—even wooly mammoth tusks, bones, and hides. In the future, just as we found substitutes for the wooly mammoth materials, we will find substitutes for any of our current favorites that run short. We can in fact expect to see far more imaginative alternatives than in the past, as technology continues to advance at an ever greater pace.

Of course, the biggest single component of housing construction costs is labor. But with the productivity of labor in manufacturing growing, again thanks to technological progress, at roughly 2% a year, these costs too should decline substantially as a fraction of our incomes.

There are some concerns that shortages of energy or water may inhibit the construction of new homes. To the extent that that is so, it argues for investing in energy or water supplies, rather than homes, which are priced separately.

As the world develops, we are certainly going to be faced with shortages of some things. But it is hard to foresee that housing will be high on the list. The demand for housing is a demand for shelter, a space to have a family and raise children that is close to a job and schools, a place to eat and sleep in privacy. It is a demand for those services, not for any single resource such as lumber or concrete. One of the most basic lessons of economics is that when one resource becomes scarce, people will find substitutes for it. There are so many different resources available to provide construction materials that it is hard to believe that housing services will become relatively more scarce than anything else.

The public, of course, does not understand this basic economic fact. And this lack of understanding has helped produce a massive speculative bubble based on a faulty impression that we are running out of the resources used in home construction.

Massive Urban Planning

The scarcity value that homes convey is due to a perceived scarcity of urban centers. But new urban centers, new towns or cities, can be built from scratch.

The new urbanism movement, which began in the 1980s, has attempted to counter the urban sprawl that represented the chief mode of growth of the built environment in the United States and other countries for the past half century. Suburbs are built up around existing major cities; they lack effective town centers, spread out so much that they consume large amounts of land, and force residents to rely on the automobile for an increasingly difficult commute into the center city.

The new urbanism as originally conceived was often about building small town and neighborhood centers. More recently some urban theorists have stressed the need to build entirely new large urban centers. Christopher Leinberger, for example, has argued that there is a significant unmet demand for large, walkable urban centers—little Manhattans, so to speak. There is high demand, he argues, for well-designed urban centers in general, not just the existing ones. A great many persons like to live in crowded cities, where the vitality of human activity makes for a stimulating life. We are a gregarious species, and most of us are happy to confine our visits to the wilderness to a few well-planned vacations.

People appreciate living in a walkable city, where opportunities of every sort are within a pleasant stroll through an agreeable environment amidst interesting crowds. Some of the world's great cities come to mind: London, New York, Paris, Tokyo. The key idea is to build new ones, and on a large scale. This is a demand that can in fact be met. It requires only sustained and coordinated effort.

There is indeed ample historical precedent for such new urban construction. The creation of new capital cities, built from scratch in relatively rural areas, has set the example. Washington, D.C., was built in this way starting in the 1790s, and it is now a major metropolis in which property is highly valued. Brasilia, Canberra, and Islamabad were built in the same way. The high urban property values in these cities are proof of the concept: we can build vital, thriving, new urban centers away from the congestion of the existing ones.

There are an increasing number of private examples as well. One is Reston Town Center, near Washington, D.C., built by Robert E. Simon (whose initials form the first syllable of the name of the city). His efforts began in the 1960s, and the Town Center was dedicated in 1990. It is a cluster of high-rise buildings placed in what was then a rural area. It apparently has enough of the qualities of a more traditional city that real estate there has begun to command high prices. And high real estate prices will increasingly promote a supply response, with new urban areas like Reston Town Center being developed to meet demand.

There are more recent examples as well. Mesa del Sol, near Albuquerque, New Mexico, is now being built on twenty-five square miles of undeveloped land by Forest City Enterprises and Covington Capital Partners, and the plans include bringing in jobs and industries that will provide the new city with a unique character. The city will be particularly distinguished by serving as home to film and media studios. It is planned to accommodate residents from all income levels, avoiding the common modern problem of service workers who cannot afford to live in the city whose residents they serve.

In China, the new city of Dongtan is being built on an island just off the coast of Shanghai. Designed by the British firm Arup, it is planned to be home to half a million people by 2050. It will be a walkable city—indeed the plans call for conventional cars to be banned from Dongtan altogether.

When I was recently in Russia I met an executive involved with the construction of the *"sputnik*-city" of Konstantinovo, which is being built just outside Moscow. (*Sputnik* means satellite in Russian.) At twelve square miles, it is about half the size of Mesa del Sol. It too will be a carefully planned community. Coincidentally its planners are also designing it to be home for film and media studios. The Russian executive I met said that he had never heard of Mesa del Sol, yet the two cities show substantial similarities. Creative minds all over the world are looking at city congestion and doing something about it, ultimately because of the expressed demand, the existence of modern construction technology, and progress in urban design theory.

These new urban projects are part of a long-run trend that will work against accelerating home prices. It is not that there isn't a shortage of land in the places surrounding the areas most people favor today. It is instead that the history of the world has for centuries seen the development of more and more land, the more intensive use of it, and migration to exploit the availability of land in other areas and other countries. Moreover, world political history has been significantly driven by resentment of the economic inequality that arises from the privileges of property owners at the expense of others. In an effort to address that inequality, land reforms that change the laws relating to ownership have occurred with some regularity.

Indeed the subprime crisis in the United States is itself, in a sense, the result of another such land reform: the U.S. government's intensifying commitment to promote homeownership, a major theme in recent elections. The regulatory tolerance in the 1990s and 2000s of loose lending practices sprang from that policy goal. More generally, the land use restrictions that create wealth for existing landowners and homeowners by preventing new construction are politically fragile, and they tend eventually to be overturned.

At present, there is no foreseeable end to these safety valves that would justify a major home-price surge. By planning around the problems that beset major urban centers, we can create new urban centers that will be, if not quite as big as the old centers, more numerous and in many ways better. These new centers will eventually compete with the old centers and steal much of their value, bringing home prices down in those locations.

Short-Run and Long-Run Responses

There has been a peculiar tendency during this housing bubble (as with other bubbles) to regard price increases as generally good news. When I speak with news reporters of the outlook for declining home prices, I am often told that I am a Cassandra. But it is in no way bad news if home prices fall. If home prices go down relative to our incomes, we become wealthier, better able to invest in new homes. Most of us have children or even grandchildren, and they are usually more numerous than we. We care about them and about others in our society, and we want these others to be able to afford homes in the future. Scarcity is not good news—low prices are.

The idea that public policy should be aimed at validating the real estate myth, preventing a collapse in home prices from ever happening, is an error of the first magnitude. In the short run a sudden drop in home prices may indeed disrupt the economy, producing undesirable systemic effects. But, in the long run, the home-price drops are clearly a good thing.

This short run–long run paradox calls to mind an analogous paradox of Keynesian economic theory: in the short run we fear a sudden increase in the savings rate, which might trigger a recession, but in the long run we want a higher savings rate, because we need the resources for investment for the future.

We must therefore consider the short run and the long run separately, and the policy responses to the two are very different. The next chapter focuses on short-run aspects of the subprime solution; the chapter after that proposes long-run solutions.

A Bailout by Any Other Name

5

Virtually all the solutions to the subprime crisis already tried or already proposed in the United States have aspects of a bailout to them. This is true of the interest rate cuts by the Fed; the Fed's lending to troubled institutions under the auspices of the TAF, the TSLF, and the PDCF; the tax rebate checks mailed out to individuals; the extension of loan limits by the FHA; and the extension of mortgage ceilings by the government-sponsored enterprises Fannie Mae and Freddie Mac.

Let us be clear about what the word *bailout* means. Actually the term has only recently acquired prominence, and the word itself is not yet even listed in the *Oxford English Dictionary.* A bailout is a rescue by the government or another entity of an irresponsible person or entity arising from a failure to follow rules or take reasonable precautionary steps. In the popular use of the term, a parent who offers a late-night meal to a child who refused to sit down at the family dinner, and is now whining about being hungry, is offering a bailout.

The earliest use I could find of the word *bailout* in this sense, from a computer search of English-language newspapers, was in 1950, in the context of criticizing the activities of the Reconstruction Finance Corporation, established during the Great Depression to rescue failing companies by lending them money. Prior to that, the term appears to have been used exclusively to refer to the act of a pilot parachuting from an airplane in trouble.

Of course, any postcontract government action that invalidates a prior contract or expectation will be called unfair by some. In the nineteenth century the preferred expressions were the "sponge of insolvency" or "premium on hazard and overtrading." But the term *bailout* is more intense, with its suggestion of abandoning an aircraft in midflight—leaving it to crash and burn on someone else.

The term was rarely used until much more recently, and in its modern meaning it also connotes unfairness and lack of consistency. A bailout is unfair to those who, because they were more responsible, did not get into trouble and thus did not qualify for the bailout. The other child, who followed the rules and sat down to dinner at the appointed time, feels unappreciated. In the case of government financial bailouts, it is ultimately the taxpayer who is typically on the line to pay for the bailout.

The use of the term *bailout* also often seems to connote deception of one sort or another. The parent who is bailing out the one child is hoping that the other child, who followed the rules, does not notice that the disobedient child is getting special attention. The disobedient child offers a phony excuse to justify having missed dinner. The parent may accept the phony excuse in front of the other child, to justify the bailout and simply keep the peace. The pattern of behavior may even become a sort of unacknowledged secret pact between parent and pampered child. But the obedient child sees the hypocrisy, feels wronged, and may be less motivated to follow rules in the future.

When the subprime crisis prompted the Federal Reserve to cut interest rates sharply to protect failing companies, its actions were necessarily having the biggest effect on the most irresponsible or risk-taking companies, who were near failure. Cutting interest rates provides resources for them, but those resources do not magically appear. They come in part from those who are living off income from funds they have invested in short-term vehicles like money market funds or savings accounts. They will see their income decline. If the interest rate cuts ultimately result in higher inflation, then anyone who has assets denominated in currency terms will suffer. Like the parent giving more attention to the disobedient child, the Fed does not mention who will ultimately suffer as a result of the bailout.

When the subprime crisis prompted the Federal Reserve to launch its TAF in December 2007 to rescue failing depository institutions, it was again aiding some of the less responsible institutions at the expense of others. Even though it takes the form of an auction open to all depository institutions, the TAF does enable the neediest among them to gain help at rates they could not obtain in the marketplace. If the Fed auctions off enough funds—and accepts, at taxpayers risk, collateral that is so compromised, with an insufficient discount—it is clearly a bailout. Essentially the same goes for the Fed's lending programs, the TSLF and PDCF. With these, the rescue is truly historic, since for the first time since the 1930s it extends Fed bailouts beyond banks that are under the Fed's direct supervision. With these programs the Federal Reserve is offering to take as collateral for loans securities, including subprime paper, for which there is no ready market.

Obviously, if there existed a viable market offering a good price for those securities, the firms would simply sell them on that market. The Fed is offering something unavailable in the marketplace. The Fed is effectively taking a risk by investing in securities that others would not touch. That is a bailout.

Who is paying for this bailout? Of course, if the Fed never loses on this collateral no one will have to pay. But if losses on the collateral mean that there are not enough funds to cover the defaulted loans, this will be reflected in lower payments by the Fed to the federal government, hence ultimately higher taxes for individuals.

There is another sort of bailout that the Fed or other central banks may also be party to in the future. There may be a tendency for central banks to tolerate more general inflation, especially if oil prices create a stagflation. Such a policy would tend to bail out anyone whose balance sheet is compromised by reduced property prices. The bailout comes at the expense of holders of nominally denominated debt. Such central bank bailouts have a long and established history.

When the Economic Stimulus Act of 2008 was enacted, providing for the mailing of tax rebate checks to individual consumers, to stimulate them to make purchases, this was also, in a sense, a bailout. It was a bailout in part because the rebate checks were sent primarily to lower-income taxpayers, and not at all to higher-income taxpayers. The rebates will have to be paid for by higher taxes for all, predominantly those with higher incomes.

Even disregarding the fact that the rebates were not mailed to high-income taxpayers, they are ultimately a sort of trick—if not an outright deception—relying for their intended result on the inability of most recipients to realize that the rebate check today will result in higher taxes in the future. Therefore the rebate has no real effect on lifetime after-tax income, and it should have no effect on consumption by a rational, far-thinking person.

Lower-income people may rightly suspect that the rebate check is really a gift to them, one that they will never have to pay for in higher taxes in the future. They should spend the money now, expecting further bailouts in the future—and indeed this consumption effect is why the government is giving proportionally larger rebate checks to them.

When the government raised the loan limits for the FHA and the Veterans Administration, and for Fannie Mae and Freddie Mac, it sounded like a boon for troubled home buyers who could not qualify for a mortgage and for those who could not sell their homes to these buyers at a good price. But what is the ultimate source of that boon? The government is not in the business of creating wealth, merely taking it from one person and giving it to another. Who is ultimately paying for these actions?

Not surprisingly, it is again the taxpayer, and that means the losers are disproportionately those people who have prudently been staying out of the housing market bubble. These government agencies and government-sponsored enterprises are ultimately, if not always officially, backed by the U.S. government. Should these mortgages default in the future, the taxpayer may well be made to bail them out again. That is what differentiates these entities from private businesses, and what makes it clear that this is a bailout.

Why Some Bailouts Are Necessary Now

Despite the unpleasant consequences just mentioned, the principal short-term remedy for the subprime crisis is, unfortunately, some combination of bailouts. Of course, these may not work. Bailouts are focused—and focus public attention—on extreme cases, at the possible expense of the general taxpayer. While they prevent some dominoes from falling, they may also harm general confidence. The use of bailouts may be compared to trying to halt a disease epidemic by lavishing emergency care on the sickest and those nearest to death. But—given the magnitude of the subprime crisis, and the disproportionate extent to which its consequences fall on the less advantaged members of our society—bailouts must be attempted. It is this component of the subprime solution to which the rest of the chapter is devoted.

Though they rarely use the word *bailout,* governments have long been in the business of managing risk for their citizens. In his 2002 book *When All Else Fails: Government as the Ultimate Risk Manager,* David A. Moss argues that "risk management constitutes a potent and pervasive public policy in the United States. Our economy would be unrecognizable without it."* In fact, financial theorists must always take account of the underlying, unstated risk-management contract that governments around the world have with their citizens and businesses. It would be a serious theoretical mistake to neglect this ubiquitous contract.

Let's return once more to the metaphor of the child who will not eat dinner at the appointed time. Now imagine that there lives in the same house a grandparent who is suffering from a painful disease or is mentally impaired; perhaps one of the child's parents is in some emotional distress. Having a child throw a tantrum in this situation would be too emotionally draining on the whole household. A wise parent might indeed bail out the unruly child now, and think later about lessons to be learned.

The dynamics of families and nations are not entirely dissimilar. Many families have long-simmering tensions. Disagreements and resentments can be smoothed over,

*David A. Moss, *When All Else Fails: Government as the Ultimate Risk Manager* (Cambridge, Mass.: Harvard University Press, 2002), p. 1.

but they may reappear from time to time. Old memories resurface. In moments of stress, it is important to avoid harsh statements that will be remembered later—even years later—only to become a source of further conflict.

By the same token, policy makers must strive to prevent economic misfortunes that will create long-standing distrust in our economic institutions. The events of the 1930s are far behind us—at least chronologically. Though we have not forgotten them, we have reached a state of mind where they are no longer emotionally relevant.

The events that marked the start of the Great Depression set the tone for the decade to follow. People with good and apparently steady jobs were cast out and suffered a train of catastrophes, such as losing their homes to foreclosure. Some were left with so few resources that they had to take the humiliating step of standing in a bread line or showing up at a soup kitchen. Middle-aged men were reduced to selling apples on the street to try to make a living. Photographs of those lines, of those sidewalk sellers, were published in newspapers, adding to the humiliation. These images, burned into the national psyche, became symbols of the times, reflecting the shame of a generation.

The trail of evidence of financial wrongdoings led back to the early 1930s, as a huge web of investment companies began to fail. People felt wronged when the banks they had been told were sound were suddenly shuttered—especially if they had not gotten to the banks in time to withdraw their deposits and were left without recourse. Photographs of long lines of those trying to retrieve their money from failing banks provided yet another vivid image. Anger and disillusionment were added to the emotional mix.

These experiences, and the enduring images they spawned, marked a dramatic change in Americans' inner assumptions. The changes were fundamental, reflecting deep psychological distress. Frederick Lewis Allen, in his 1931 book *Only Yesterday: An Informal History of the 1920s,* remarked that "one could hardly walk a block [at the beginning of the 1930s] in any American city or town without noticing some of them."[*] Women's fashions changed: short skirts disappeared and a more formal and less provocative style emerged. Gone was the excited sense that we were entering a new era in which taboos would be abandoned. Romantic and poetic plays and novels reappeared, replacing others that had challenged contemporary values. Admiration for entrepreneurs and savvy businessmen waned. Delight in the then-shocking theories of avant-garde Freudian psychologists became less common. Even religious thinking returned to more

[*]Frederick Lewis Allen, *Only Yesterday: An Informal History of the 1920s* (New York: Harper and Brothers, 1931), p. 289.

traditional forms. The public amusement at religious foibles so evident at the time of the 1925 Scopes trial, when the Bible was put on trial versus the theory of evolution, was fading, and being replaced by a desire to find in religion some comforting interpretation of life.

In 1932 psychiatrist W. Beran Wolfe wrote that a "psychological pall has settled over the whole country.... The unemployed American sits at home, listens to his radio if he has not been dispossessed, stands humbly in a bread line, applies apologetically to a social agency for relief, and, if refused, submits to the most intolerable human indignities. Slave morality has returned."*

In the 1930s radical sentiment intensified. In his 1968 book *The Heyday of American Communism: The Depression Decade,* Harvey Klehr detailed how Americans, both workers and intellectuals, began to be won over to communist theories; the 1930s have been called the "Red decade." Labor-management relations deteriorated into hostility, and labor disputes were unusually intense, sometimes becoming violent. In terms of threats to economic confidence, the current subprime crisis in some ways resembles the onset of the Great Depression.

In his 2007 book *La crise des années 1930 est devant nous,* François Lenglet, the editor of the French business

---

*W. Beran Wolfe, "Psychoanalyzing the Depression," *Forum and Century* 87(4): 209–15, 1932.

magazine *Les Echos,* sees parallels in the changes in values and customs and in the loss of confidence, even the onset of despair, all reflecting a descent from the euphoria of the bubble years. In good times people are willing to cooperate and accommodate others, but when optimism for the future starts to sour, they can become introverted, angry, fearful, and selfish.

Benjamin Friedman, in his 2005 book *The Moral Consequences of Economic Growth,* cites evidence from world history that, at times when people see encouraging prospects for the future, they are better able to work together constructively, supporting democratic principles and political and social liberalization. When perceived prospects for growth falter, there are major setbacks.

Friedman points out that in much of the world, particularly Europe, the Great Depression of the 1930s demonstrated all the consequences that his theory would predict: the rise of fascism, anti-Semitism, racism, nationalism, and eventually the outbreak of World War II. But the United States in the 1930s, he claims, "stands out as an exception—in many respects *the* exception"—to his theory.* Somehow a spirit of cooperation and change developed here, ultimately embodied in the New Deal; while there was great unrest, there was also a sense of

---

*Benjamin M. Friedman, *The Moral Consequences of Economic Growth* (New York: Knopf, 2005), p. 159.

positive institutional change and progress, which offset the despair of the Depression. Hostility between labor and management, and between rich and poor, was tempered by the sense that we were all moving together toward a more enlightened world.

According to Klehr, the sharp increase in communist sympathies in the United States in the 1930s was halted by two principal factors: the Roosevelt administration's aggressive actions to deal with the communists' very complaints and the 1939 Nazi-Soviet pact, which forever discredited communism in the eyes of most Americans. While the latter was a purely external event, the former was a matter of deliberate action by U.S. policy makers. A notable milestone occurred in May 1933, when First Lady Eleanor Roosevelt waded through ankle-deep mud to visit the communist-inspired Second Bonus Army, encamped outside Washington, D.C. She addressed them with such personal warmth that her remarks were interpreted as evidence of the administration's sympathy with and willingness to act on the group's concerns, if not their immediate demands.

The differing reactions to the Depression in the United States and Europe had an earlier parallel in the response to the end of World War I. We can see this clearly from the evidence presented in *The Economic Consequences of the Peace* by John Maynard Keynes. The arguments by the victorious allies for heavy reparations from defeated Germany were made without regard for the damage, economic and otherwise, that these conditions would inflict on that country and on national sentiments among both victors and vanquished. Keynes wrote: "Will France be safe because her sentries stand on the Rhine, if her own finances are in ruinous disorder, if she is spiritually isolated from her friends, if bloodshed, misery and fanaticism prevail from the Rhine eastward through two continents?"*

History proves that Keynes was right to worry about the social changes brought on by the unfortunate economic arrangements of that time, for they would be among the causes of World War II a generation later. We must always be concerned about public perceptions of fairness and evenhanded treatment, about public confidence that our economic system is moving forward to provide opportunities for all. That confidence is being seriously eroded in today's subprime crisis.

We are at risk that reaction to the current economic crisis could set us far back, economically as well as socially. We must act now to prevent even the possibility that a severe crisis could endanger our comity. Just as less-developed countries need to prevent the global food

*John Maynard Keynes, *The Economic Consequences of the Peace* (London: Macmillan, 1919), p. xi.

crisis from endangering the least fortunate people there, so too must advanced countries live up to their duties to protect their own least fortunate. The loss of trust and belief in the economic system can have consequences not only for the economy itself, but for the social fabric as a whole, leading us all to suffer needlessly.

The immediate fix that is needed is similar to that called for by the Great Depression. In the words of Henry B. Steagall, chairman of the House Banking and Currency Committee, in 1932, "Of course, it involves a departure from established policies and ideals, but we cannot stand by when a house is on fire to engage in lengthy debates over the methods to be employed in extinguishing the fire. In such a situation we instinctively seize upon and utilize whatever method is most available and offers assurance of speediest success."[*]

The fire analogy is an apt one, since the real problem we were facing then, and are facing now, is a sort of conflagration—a problem that spreads rapidly from person to person and business to business. The more serious consequences of the subprime crisis fall into the category of "systemic effects"—effects that will be felt throughout the entire economic system. In medicine, the systemic effects of a trauma are those that involve the whole body,

---

[*]"Henry B. Steagall Tells How New Body Will Aid Business," *New York Times*, January 24, 1932, p. 26.

including parts that were distant from the initial trauma. For example, an injury to a limb leads it to become gangrenous, and this will result in death unless the affected limb is amputated.

In economics, systemic effects are all about *externalities,* especially those that show up in extreme circumstances. Often these systemic effects on the economy have to do with investor confidence and psychological or social contagion. The classic example is a nationwide bank run spurred by the failure of a single bank or a small number of banks. When depositors even suspect that they might lose their money, they may withdraw their money from all banks. Even the soundest banks maintain only a fraction of the reserves that would be needed to meet such a catastrophic demand. Fractional-reserve banking involves multiple equilibria: People trust their banks, and thus the banks come to be seen as trustworthy. But, conversely, if people lose trust in their banks, withdraw their funds, and cause the banks to fail, the lack of trust has become a self-fulfilling prophesy. The jump from one equilibrium to the other is still not easily understood, since it encompasses social contagion as well as economic contagion.

The onset of the Great Depression of the 1930s, which followed the stock market crash of 1929 and infected the United States and other advanced countries around the world, was such a systemic failure. The crisis actually began before 1929—in the housing market. Only later did it spread to the stock market, then triggering a severe banking crisis that had repercussions for almost all businesses.

Economic historian Christina Romer has argued that the onset of the Great Depression of the 1930s coincided with adverse public reaction to the stock market crash of 1929. She finds that forecasters reacted to the economic effects of that crash very differently than they had to the economic downturns of 1920–21 and 1923–24. Right after the 1929 crash, the forecasters, although they did not predict the depression that was to follow, expressed unusual *uncertainty* about the economic outlook. Romer believes that it was this uncertainty that led to the sharp contraction in consumer spending that ultimately caused the Depression.

An economic downturn can ultimately change the nature of political support for economic policies—even to the point of exacerbating the downturn. One consequence of the strengthening of pro-labor sentiment during the Depression, as argued by economists Harold Cole and Lee Ohanian, is that government policy encouraged firms to accede to union demands, even if those demands were really for the benefit of insiders and at the expense of the outsiders—those who were currently unemployed. The National Industrial Recovery Act of 1933, one of the less inspired innovations of the New Deal, gave the president the power to allow firms to collude on prices so long as they raised wages and accepted unions. Even after the act was declared unconstitutional in 1935, the Roosevelt administration continued to be lenient in bringing antitrust actions against firms that were compliant with union demands.

There is today the possibility of what, in *Irrational Exuberance,* I called an attention cascade, leading us to start worrying about possible economic problems that had left our consciousness. In an attention cascade, economic events or problems become the subject of more and more talk and of stories in the media, until they come to dominate public thinking. The changes are qualitative—taking the form of greater salience of certain stories, theories, and facts—and are not measured by the various consumer confidence indices that are so widely disseminated. In fact long-lasting and severe changes can take place before conventional economists have any clue about them.

The subprime crisis was not on the list of possible scenarios for which we might have made plans. We are stuck with contractual arrangements that were made in error. Although many were clearly lured into financial deep water by the prospect of easy money and quick riches when they should have exercised greater prudence, others are in trouble through no fault of their own and are resorting to desperate fixes. Much as we might like to, we cannot quickly and reliably sort out who is at fault and who is not.

I emphasize that the possible *systemic effects* are much more important than the loss of home values in a potential collapse of the real estate market. For however much home values may drop, they will still remain the same homes, offering the same services to all of us. But if the rate of output in the economy falls, that is a real loss, not just a paper one. The balance sheet problems into which people fall if their homes lose value are purely financial losses. But they can be converted into substantial *real* losses to the economy if they are allowed to destroy public confidence.

In a financial system seize-up such as the one we are now experiencing, we must, putting aside our political and policy differences, fall back immediately on a more basic social contract—one that dictates that we as a society will protect everyone from major misfortune and keep existing problems from spreading further, subject to the dictates of common sense. That social contract is our most valuable protection, for we as a society can never plan for all possible contingencies.

Indeed bailouts of one sort of another have been part of the underlying stabilization mechanism of economies, ours as well as those of other countries, for centuries. The Federal Reserve has been bailing out troubled banks since it opened for business in 1914. The Bank of England has been doing the same for hundreds of years. We must face up to the fact that we have not been able to avoid bailouts in the past, and we cannot do so today.

While it is natural to emphasize the unfairness of bailouts to those who do not receive them, judgments of what is fair and unfair are far from clear-cut. There is an inherent unfairness in our economy, evidenced by its sharp income inequalities. Some of this represents vestigial effects of injustices of long ago, notably the importation of blacks to the United States as slaves. To this day, black Americans as a group have not completely managed to shake off the economic aftereffects of this history of oppression.

The FHA, as well as such government-sponsored enterprises as Fannie Mae and Freddie Mac, in their role as subsidizers of housing for those with low incomes, can be viewed as rectifying at least some of the income inequality in our society. Moreover, subsidizing low-income housing probably has positive social externalities whose value is incalculable. There is a better prospect for social harmony if some of the more marginal members of our society feel invested in its success through ownership of their own homes. If this is a time for increased bailouts of those with low incomes, then maybe that is all to the good. Perhaps the subprime crisis is sharpening our social conscience, if only in indirect ways.

A New Home Owners' Loan Corporation

We need a new organization modeled after the Home Owners' Loan Corporation that was established in 1933, during the last major housing crisis, to make credit more readily available to home borrowers. By the time this book reaches print, there is a chance we will already have some aspects of such an organization in place or at least in the works. Plans along these lines enjoy strong support, including the backing of economists such as Alan Blinder and Martin Feldstein and legal scholars such as Michael Barr. Yet the prospect of congressional action on this proposal remains highly controversial, and it is best considered as still nothing more than a proposal. Any action eventually taken by Congress may be watered down or handled ineffectively, and, even if it does act meaningfully, Congress may not respond in the future with sufficient additional funds for the institution if the subprime crisis worsens.

The HOLC accepted mortgages as collateral for loans to mortgage lenders, so long as the mortgages had more enlightened terms than were customary at the time. In that way the HOLC both dealt with the immediate problem of foreclosures and also encouraged longer-term economic innovation. That is what a new HOLC can and should do today.

It is essential that the potential cost of bailouts be paid by the broad public, and that it not be dumped into the laps of a small set of investors. Ben Bernanke has been widely described as asking our nation's bankers to write down the principal on millions of mortgage loans. What he *really* said was that principal writedowns "could be in the best interest of both borrowers and lenders."* Of course, some limited writedowns are in the interest of lenders: if a lender fails to improve the mortgage terms for a troubled homeowner, then the owner may simply abandon the property, often in damaged condition, thus imposing substantial legal costs and delays on the lender. Lenders understand very well that it is in their own interest to keep homeowners in place if there is reasonable hope they can pay on somewhat reduced terms. Bernanke is rightfully concerned that his language not suggest that some unfortunate group of investors should bear the cost of dealing with systemic effects on the U.S. economy. But by limiting his attention to actions that would mutually benefit borrowers and lenders, he is proposing only that lenders should continue to do what they already do. His

---

*Ben S. Bernanke, "Reducing Preventable Mortgage Foreclosures," speech at the Independent Community Bankers of America Annual Convention, Orlando, Florida, March 4, 2008, http://www .federalreserve.gov/newsevents/speech/bernanke20080304a.htm.

talk is not effective in dealing with the subprime crisis because it carries no economic weight.

U.S. Senator Christopher Dodd (D-CT) proposed a federal Homeownership Preservation Corporation that would be a modern-day version of the HOLC. Dodd later dropped the idea of such a new corporation, but in a press conference he and U.S. Representative Barney Frank (D-MA) together spoke of empowering the FHA to guarantee up to $300 billion in refinanced mortgages to distressed borrowers. They did not describe this as a bailout or a burden on taxpayers—but of course it has the potential to become one if default rates turn out to be high.

It may be better to create a new agency, like Dodd's now-withdrawn Homeownership Preservation Corporation, rather than merely extend the financing of the FHA, because a new organization is more likely to do more than just funnel money to mortgage lenders. A new agency is more likely to attract leaders interested in fundamental change; creating such an agency is a way of signaling serious intent to solve the subprime problem. We need to see other aspects of the HOLC solution implemented now as well. In particular we need to see our reborn HOLC establish new mortgage-writing conventions, as I discuss in the next chapter.

Getting the Short-Run Solutions Right

Just as important as the specific short-run solutions to be implemented is the underlying mindset. We must get these solutions right, and get them right the first time. This means facing up to the scope of the problem, allocating sufficient resources to solving it, and setting the correct fundamental policy goals.

If any of the short-run solutions discussed here are to have a chance of success, our leaders must, in the first place, admit that a serious problem exists. It does not help matters if leaders continually assert that a turnaround is just around the corner. That was the strategy played by Herbert Hoover during the Great Depression, and it has been trotted out by virtually every leader in government and business since then when faced with the necessity of truly fundamental reform. Such an attitude only leads to accusations that those in charge are attempting to manipulate the public mind through the power of suggestion.

We have to be ready for the possibility that many more tax rebates will be necessary, perhaps for years to come. These rebates may eventually have a significant negative impact on the national debt. That possibility can be accepted only if we truly recognize the seriousness of the problem.

We need to pay attention as well to the capital adequacy of banks and broker-dealers, who are likely to come under increasing pressure if, as is likely, there are continued substantial falls in home prices, further impairing their assets. Their inadequate capitalization will be evident to everyone with whom they do business, and this will lead to further freeze-ups of the system, which may spread rapidly in a worsening crisis.

We must be willing to devote sufficient resources to doing the bailouts right. Leaders should face the fact that they are bailouts and get on with carefully and calmly explaining the reason for them. Only then can enough money be spent on them to have the desired effects.

Setting the proper policy focus is also crucial. The purpose of the bailouts should *not* be to maintain high values in the housing market, the stock market, or any other speculative market. The essential purpose is to prevent a fundamental loss of economic confidence in our institutions and in each other, and to maintain a sense of social justice. As such, the bailouts should focus most intensely on preventing distress among people of modest means.

With regard to housing prices, government policy should be just the opposite of supporting them. We need more planned large urban centers, and building more of these would increase supply and thereby bring urban home prices down. The framers of the 1968 Housing and Urban Development Act understood this need, and the act set up a mechanism whereby builders of whole new towns could apply to the Department of Housing and Urban Development for support. That legislation has led to some new urban centers, but the act was not enough, and legislation is needed to support development of new urban communities.

In terms of the immediate crisis, the problem is quite different. We have to be willing to spend money on securing economic justice. That means allocating resources to determining—to the extent that this is possible—who among mortgage borrowers were misled and mistreated, and then focusing the bailouts on them.

Certain nonprofit organizations, such as Self-Help (www.self-help.org) or the Neighborhood Assistance Corporation of America (www.naca.com) provide for assistance to individual homeowners to help them work things out. But the resources of these organizations are dwarfed by the scale of the current crisis. The government's Hope Now initiative is failing to provide enough solutions because it really has no official resources; it is merely a government-led alliance of businesses. If home prices continue to fall, many more homeowners will be in trouble in the coming years, amounting to a very expensive problem and putting even more stress on an already inadequate system.

The government can spend money now to reorganize the system of bailouts so that it operates on a more systematic basis. A new HOLC could tackle the expensive and complex process of modifying individual loans, rewarding those mortgage lenders who will spend the time and energy to help individual borrowers understand their specific situations and make government assistance available to those who qualify.

After we have succeeded in preventing the subprime crisis from escalating, we must turn to the long-term solutions that will prevent a recurrence of the situation in which we find ourselves. That aspect of the subprime solution is the subject of the next chapter.

The Promise of Financial Democracy

The key to the subprime solution, to preventing future crises like the current one, as well as mitigating its after-effects, is democratizing finance—extending the application of sound financial principles to a larger and larger segment of society, and using all the modern technology at our disposal to achieve that goal.

Doing this will reduce the long-run incidence of speculative bubbles like the housing bubble that we have just experienced. And to the extent that such bubbles still occur, it will establish a rational context for responding to them, instead of the after-the-fact scurrying for quick fixes that we have seen since the onset of the subprime crisis in 2007.

There used to be tremendous instability in the banking sector. For example, there were severe U.S. banking crises in 1797, 1819, 1837, 1857, 1873, 1893, 1907, and 1933. Those problems were largely fixed by a number of institutional changes over the years, notably the creation of the Federal Reserve System in 1913 and the New Deal reforms of the early 1930s. But effective reforms haven't reached all segments of our economy, especially the household sector, which continues to limp along with practically medieval financial insight. Unless we think more broadly about financial reforms that will encompass the majority of households, we will continue to experience crises.

As the events leading up to the subprime crisis make plain, it is remarkable that the imperfections of our basic economic institutions have not been more widely discussed. While markets bubble and burst, most people have only minimal protections against their biggest economic risks, hold dangerously undiversified portfolios, and risk ruin when they lose their jobs or fall ill.

These problems are regarded as inevitable features of the system, and the system itself is considered impervious to reform, as if it were a product of nature. But successful institutional reform efforts such as those of the New Deal era belie this widely held orthodoxy. Basic institutional reform is not only possible but necessary.

The subprime crisis has revealed a poverty of imagination on the part of leaders in initiating the reforms needed to build the new institutional foundations for a more secure economic environment. This chapter suggests ways of beginning just such an institutional reform initiative.

It's the Technology

Institutional reform starts with understanding the available technology. *Information technology* is the story of our time. It is key to the subprime solution. The continued growth of computers, data collection and processing capabilities, "smart" technology, and rapid, inexpensive communications all provide dramatically effective tools to implement the subprime solution—to correct some of the egregious faults in the economy's institutional foundation.

Along with this expanding information technology, there has been over recent decades a magnificent development of our knowledge in the field of mathematical finance. The field has captured the imaginations of mathematically inclined people, from traditional economics departments, to mathematics departments, to management schools, and now to engineering schools with their new financial engineering programs, and to numerous quant groups at investment banks and hedge funds. This theory, as part of economics, in turn allows us to harness the full potential of risk-management technology—especially when it is implemented on a sufficiently large scale, as our information technology now allows. The theoretical advances are important, for they tell us where and how to look for opportunities to use financial technology to advance human welfare.

Mathematical finance theory helps us understand how *both* sides of a financial contract can benefit from the contract, and it suggests how we can optimize the participation of the two sides so that human welfare as a whole is enhanced. We must rely on such theory if we are to avoid inconsistent and erratic policy proposals to deal with crises, such as capriciously awarding bailouts to some without properly considering the context, the appropriate incentives, or who is on "the other side," paying for the bailouts.

Modern financial theory has as an important component in *agency theory*. Agency theory explains how to motivate agents to behave as much as possible in the interests of *all* parties to a transaction, not just themselves. It is a theory that explains how to keep moral hazard under control by structuring financial institutions with just the right balance of incentives.

In a similar vein, the human sciences—psychology, sociology, anthropology, and neurobiology—are increasing our understanding of the mind by leaps and bounds, and this knowledge is now being applied to finance and economics. We have a much better grasp of how and why people make economic errors, and of how we can restructure institutions to help avoid these errors.

There has been an important revolution with the development, in the past few decades, of the field of behavioral economics, including behavioral finance. This discipline incorporates insights gained in other social sciences. For that reason, many financial theorists of the old school have resisted this revolution, for they fear that it renders their mathematical models useless. On the contrary—it opens up their models to far richer and more successful applications.

Denying the importance of psychology and other social sciences for financial theory would be analogous to physicists denying the importance of friction in the application of Newtonian mechanics. If one is permitted to apply Newtonian mechanics only in realms where friction can be completely disregarded, then one is confining its application largely to astronomy. Once we add a theory of friction, Newtonian mechanics can begin to be applied to earthly problems as well, and it becomes an essential tool for engineers who are designing devices to improve our daily lives. We have a comparable opportunity today with the advent of behavioral economics, which has the potential to facilitate exciting advances in *financial* engineering.

New institutions can be developed to solve many of the world's fundamental risk problems. But, as noted previously, this can be achieved only if the institutional foundations are retrofitted to produce greater economic growth through steadily expanded asset ownership—especially homeownership.

What follows is a package of proposed reforms that leaders—government, civic, and business, both here and abroad—can forge into a new institutional foundation for the housing market and other asset markets. Taken together, these proposed measures resonate with the spirit and letter of the reforms introduced during the New Deal era as a response to the financial failures of the 1930s, and with other institutional reform initiatives, such as the Basel II reforms deployed to secure today's international banking system.

Since these proposals in some cases represent significant departures from established practice, there will be those who will doubt that they can ever be put into practice. But we have to remember that the history of finance is one of periodic major breakthroughs in method and form. These breakthroughs have often happened at times of financial crisis, just as the innovations of the New Deal era occurred during the Great Depression. And the time for further institutional innovations is now right.

The changes proposed here are significant, but a number of them have been tried on a smaller scale, and all are distinctly within the realm of possibility. The net effect of this package of reforms would be to stress-proof the whole economy, building greater ballast into the institutional framework so that buyers and sellers are better able to conduct business with confidence rather than through desperate speculative moves.

A New Information Infrastructure

Promoting an improved information infrastructure—the knowledge base used by people and firms to manage their financial affairs—is not only good policy but also good economics. According to economic theory, information that is freely available is a public good, which tends to be undersupplied by the private sector. Moreover, the lack of information can have systemic effects, a negative externality that government should try to prevent. Strengthening the information infrastructure would have a fundamental impact in altering the social contagion and information cascades that underlie the formation of speculative bubbles.

Government promotion of a fundamentally improved information infrastructure can capitalize on the advances we have made in recent years in both information technology and behavioral economics. Thus far some apparently promising innovations in information technology have proven unsatisfactory in practice because they have not been properly human-engineered. For example, public use of financial planning web sites, the financial engines, while growing, is still not widespread. This is probably the case because people tend not to take action on important financial matters based on information that is provided to them only by computer. They must talk to a person before they make major changes in their financial behavior. Behavioral economics offers many such lessons for the proper use of information technology.

In this section I consider six major ways of improving the information infrastructure: promoting comprehensive financial advice, establishing a consumer-oriented government financial watchdog, adopting default conventions and standards that work well for most individuals, improving the disclosure of information regarding financial securities, creating large national databases of fine-grained data pertaining to individuals' economic situations, and creating a new system of economic units of measurement.

Comprehensive Financial Advice

Low-income individuals who took out risky subprime mortgages, with interest rates that would soon be adjusted upward, were often unaware of the known risks inherent in such mortgages. They had no clue that there was a real risk that, in the event of a crisis, they would not be able to refinance their mortgages. Why not? Because there was little economic impetus to provide such information through established communication channels. Thus these new homeowners unwittingly assumed hazardous risks.

Financial advice magazines did indeed report on these risks. So, while the higher-income subscribers to those publications got the story and stuck overwhelmingly to conventional fixed-rate mortgages, many lower-income people were left with personal tragedies.

The first step in correcting this failure of public education is to promote comprehensive financial advice for everyone through institutions that will make sure that all individuals, not just the most wealthy, receive such advice. Most financial advisers ignore middle- to lower-income customers because they can make money only by charging a fee based on the fraction of assets under management or by receiving commissions contingent on the purchase or sale of a security—income available only through servicing wealthier clients. As part of their efforts to operate efficiently and profitably, many financial advisers also streamline their practices, limiting their advice to narrow windows, such as portfolio management advice or tax strategies.

Most people *need* broad elementary financial advice, and they need to get it from knowledgeable and trustworthy sources. Unfortunately only wealthier people feel they can *afford* such advice.

The alternative is for financial advisers to offer their services for a flat hourly fee, in much the same way as do other professionals, such as lawyers or accountants. The National Association of Personal Financial Advisors has a sound approach to the problem. It requires its member advisers to sign a fiduciary oath not to accept remuneration from third parties for the sale of financial products or for referrals. But it remains a relatively small organization. Meanwhile, most other financial advisers have resisted the move to fee-only practices, for the simple reason that there is not enough demand for such services at the prices they would have to charge.

As a result, low-income people are left with only biased sources of advice. For example, when they are home buyers, they typically deal with a real estate agent and a mortgage broker. The real estate agent represents the seller of the house and thus has an incentive to make the sale happen at a good price for the seller. The mortgage broker has an incentive to arrange a loan that carries a high interest rate. Moreover, mortgage brokers who may appear to be helping their clients obtain a mortgage at the best rate are often, unknown to those clients, collecting fees from the lenders.

The U.S. government in effect subsidizes financial advice by making it tax deductible. But this tax deduction works only to encourage high-income people to seek out financial advice. People in low tax brackets do not benefit significantly from itemized deductions and thus usually do not itemize. Moreover, the deduction for financial advice is a miscellaneous deduction, which, even for those who do itemize, is deductible only to the extent that the sum of such deductions exceeds 2% of adjusted gross income. Thus low-income taxpayers have little or no tax incentive to pay for financial advice.

The government needs to reverse this bias and effectively subsidize fee-only, comprehensive, independent financial advice for everyone. One way to do this would be to set up a co-pay arrangement like that already in place for Medicare, Medicaid, and private health insurance plans, under which the practitioner can apply for partial reimbursement of fees. The analogy to health insurance is apt: we need both medical and financial advice on an ongoing basis, and failure to obtain either ultimately imposes costs on society when our health—medical or financial—suffers. Another form of subsidy would be to switch the current incentive for financial advice from an itemized deduction to a refundable tax credit that is obtainable upon filing one's income tax return, even if one does not choose to itemize.

Qualification for the subsidy should require that the adviser sign a statement that he or she will accept no other remuneration from third parties for this customer, so that the advice rendered is impartial. Professionals who collect commissions for selling financial products are certainly providing a helpful service, for otherwise many useful products would not reach their intended markets. But their commissions—and their current tax deductibility on personal income taxes via basis calculations for capital gains—ought to be incentive enough for them to pursue such commission-based sales without having their fees further subsidized by the government.

What if, when they were buying their homes in the run-up to the subprime crisis, low-income people had had access to good-quality, comprehensive financial advice, delivered to them one-on-one, Suze Orman–style, by trusted advisers? The crisis might never have occurred. While the true magnitude and extent of the housing bubble may not have been apparent to many financial advisers as it was happening, most of them must at least have had some sense that the housing boom might not continue. Surely they would have known when a low-income family was taking on excessive risk with an adjustable-rate mortgage or a mortgage that was simply too large for their income.

Another example, from after the bursting of the bubble, will illustrate the necessity for financial advice that springs from a pure incentive to help the client, and compensation based solely on the time taken to do so. Today, with falling home prices, many elderly people who need care and special services are postponing moving to a continuing care retirement community (CCRC) because they are unwilling to accept the loss of value of their homes if they sell now. They need to sell their houses before they can move into a CCRC, in order to be able to pay the entrance fees, but they are worrying about the decline in home prices and are thus deferring this important step. Many of them will hold out for years, hoping to sell their homes at a better price, and this trend is already being reflected in high vacancy rates in CCRCs today. Thus these elderly homeowners may go for years without proper care, often in isolation and loneliness. All they really need is to have a trusted counselor, expert in the specialty of elder finance, who will, for an hourly fee, consider all aspects of their situation—including health needs and tax consequences—and put things into perspective. Losing, say, $30,000 on the quick sale of a house in a slow market may in the final analysis be the right thing to do, given their other concerns.

There is, of course, the question of how many will actually avail themselves of financial advice, even if its cost is reduced considerably. We will only know the answer if we set the subsidy in place. If we provide the impetus for a new financial advice industry by subsidizing it, the hope is that its practitioners will find new marketing strategies, new delivery channels for their advice, or new means of bundling their advice with other products and services—strategies designed to induce people who have never before done so to start using personalized financial advice.

If government makes the business of providing such useful and impartial advice economically viable by subsidizing it, then it is likely that business will make the necessary investments to deploy new information technology on a significantly expanded scale. The provision of low-cost financial advice would be a natural application for such technology. The financial engine web sites will be reinvented so that they operate hand-in-hand with the personal advice furnished by advisers, and thus work effectively for most people. These sites might further evolve, wiki-style, into places where people can share financial information with each other and with a variety of experts.

If we reform our tax policy to subsidize the services of fee-only, comprehensive financial advisers, technology will carry us forward into new dimensions of democratized financial sophistication that we cannot now imagine.

A New Financial Watchdog

The second step in correcting the inadequacies of our information infrastructure, as outlined by legal scholar Elizabeth Warren, would be for the government to set up what she calls a financial product safety commission, modeled after the Consumer Product Safety Commission. Its primary mission would be to protect the financial consumer, to serve as an ombudsman and advocate. It would provide a resource for information on the safety of financial products and impose regulations to ensure such safety. Remarkably, such concern for the safety of financial products is not the primary charge of any major financial regulatory agency in the United States today.

The National Highway Traffic Safety Administration maintains data on highway and motor vehicle safety and statistics on accidents. In the same way, we must fund a government organization empowered to accumulate information on the actual experience that individuals have with financial products—and the "accidents," rare as well as commonplace, that happen with them—with an eye toward preventing such accidents in the future.

The U.S. Treasury's 2008 *Blueprint for a Modernized Financial Regulatory Structure* (Henry Paulson, Richard Steel, and David Nason) proposed a business-conduct regulator that resembles Warren's financial product safety commission. The proposal emphasized that the domains of regulatory authorities should be defined in terms of their objectives—and consumer protection is indeed plausible as the domain for a separate regulatory agency.

Default-Option Financial Planning

The third step in renovating the information infrastructure is to set up standardized default-option financial plans that operate well when people are inattentive and fail to act. A default option is the choice that is automatically made if an individual fails to make an intentional choice among available options. One might say that the fundamental cause of the subprime crisis was that many people simply did not pay attention. They fell into traps of one sort or another because they did not know or understand what was happening in the marketplace. When their attention lapses, consumers are more likely to accept whatever financial contract is offered first, or seems standard or conventional. Therefore designing standard contracts, including prudent default options, should be a serious enterprise for both government and business. Careful research has revealed how immensely susceptible people are to whatever they see as standard provisions in their decisions about investments.

The economist Brigitte Madrian and her colleagues studied how individuals choose whether to participate in an employer-sponsored retirement savings plan. They found that automatic enrollment of the employee in a retirement plan boosts participation immensely, even if the employee is free to drop the plan at any time by merely asking to opt out. Moreover, employees in these plans typically accept the default-option contribution rate and portfolio allocation that are built into the plans. Because of such research, the U. S. Congress decided to encourage such plans, and the Pension Protection Act of 2006 paved the way for widespread adoption of such plans.

Richard Thaler and Shlomo Benartzi have argued for a "Save More Tomorrow" plan that deducts from paychecks automatically from any increases in pay for deposit into a saving plan, and this helps overcome employee inertia in starting a saving plan.* Their plan also received a boost from the Pension Protection Act of 2006, and has now been adopted by thousands of employers.

The government can do much more along these lines to encourage the ultimate democratization of finance. The help of the government is needed as a facilitator of progress in the private sector. I noted in Chapter 1 that one of the great innovations to come out of the housing crisis of the Great Depression was the extension of mortgage terms from the then-common period of five years to fifteen years or more, providing borrowers with a greater cushion of time to pay off their mortgages. The change was made by the Home Owners' Loan Corporation in 1933, and, while that government-sponsored enterprise no longer exists, its legacy lives on today in the form of long-term mortgages. Why didn't the private sector make the adjustment itself, without government intervention? The answer apparently lies in the difficulty of introducing new products in the face of initial buyer resistance and entrenched social norms. The cost of educating the public about the wisdom of a new form of mortgage is a type of public good, yet the private firm

---

*Richard Thaler and Shlomo Benartzi, "Save More Tomorrow™: Using Behavioral Economics to Increase Saving," *Journal of Political Economy* 112(S1):S164–S187, 2004.

that incurs it may never fully recoup the cost, since the benefits will be shared by all firms that choose to offer the new mortgage.

This calls for the authoritative assertion of new standard boilerplate for common contracts such as mortgages. Most individuals will accept a standard contract if it is put forward by those whom they consider experts, and they will not try to judge the issues for themselves. A new HOLC could, as we shall discuss below, make improved mortgage contracts the standard by accepting as collateral for loans to mortgage lenders only mortgages including the new features. Such a standard-setting enterprise by the new HOLC would in turn be likely to drive an array of other financial innovations, such as the development of derivative markets for income risks and home-price risks.

In the subprime crisis many mortgage borrowers blandly accepted the mortgage terms that were offered them, in many cases likely thinking that these somehow had the imprimatur of experts—even when no consumer protections whatsoever were in place. Changing the standard mortgage contract would thus constitute a huge improvement in the information infrastructure. And reform in this area might encourage a concerted effort by experts in business and government to decide on other kinds of financial advice and improved mortgage products that could be made standard and generic for most people, thereby democratizing the information available to consumers. Other mortgage products could certainly still be developed, for those borrowers who might take the initiative to go beyond the default option.

Another possible default option would be a requirement that every mortgage borrower have the assistance of a professional akin to a civil law notary. Such notaries practice in many countries, although not in the United States. In Germany, for example, the civil law notary is a trained legal professional who reads aloud and interprets the contract and provides legal advice to both parties before witnessing their signatures. This approach particularly benefits those who fail to obtain competent and objective legal advice. The participation of such a government-appointed figure in the mortgage lending process would make it more difficult for unscrupulous mortgage lenders to steer their clients toward sympathetic lawyers, who would not adequately warn the clients of the dangers they could be facing.

Improved Financial Disclosure

The fourth step in enhancing the information infrastructure is to improve the disclosure of information that is relevant to people's financial and economic lives. Apparently almost no one had an economic incentive to do the investigative work to unearth and interpret information about the off-balance-sheet accounting that eventually doomed the Enron Corporation in 2001. Nor was there anyone with an economic incentive to reveal the excesses of the structured investment vehicles that banks were using to move certain risks off their balance sheets before the 2007 crisis. Word never got out in a way that was useful to the broad public.

Those who bought residential-mortgage-backed securities based on subprime mortgages typically did so with little more information than that contained in the ratings given them by rating agencies. And while the rating agencies themselves release additional information, the ratings are the only easily interpreted and compared pieces of information, and even these are released only with caveats.

When John Moody in 1915 offered to the public the securities rating system (with letter grades like Aaa) he was making an early step toward democratizing finance by providing a reader-friendly disclosure of information. Disclosure of financial information took another step forward in the United States in 1934 with the creation of the Securities and Exchange Commission. The SEC now sponsors a web site called EDGAR that provides detailed information on public securities and the companies that issue them, including real-time access to filings made with the SEC. When SEC Chairman Arthur Levitt in the late 1990s brought plain English into securities documentation he too was democratizing finance and improving disclosure. The effectiveness of that disclosure was further enhanced in 2000 with the SEC's issuance of Regulation Fair Disclosure (Regulation FD), which directed firms to post their announcements electronically and immediately, thus making material information available at the same time to all investors, large and small.

Despite the significant strides the SEC has made in making information available to the public, however, people still find it very difficult to evaluate the risk of securities. Thus the subprime residential-mortgage-backed securities were grossly misjudged because no one outside the rating agencies understood the information to correctly gauge the soundness of the mortgages on which they were based. The stage was perfectly set for unscrupulous mortgage originators to lend to low-income people who were likely to default, and for mortgage securitizers to sell the soon-to-default mortgages off to unsuspecting investors.

There have been important proposals for enhanced disclosure, but there has been little action.* Both govern-

*Enhancing Disclosure in the Mortgage-Backed Securities Markets, SEC Staff Report, 2003.

ment regulators and private information providers have to think much further how we can provide real understanding to the public about securities. As information technology continues to advance, the costs of providing information continue to fall, and the scope for creative and meaningful disclosure, at constant or even declining cost, should generally widen over time.

This means developing creative new presentation modes, going beyond the traditional securities ratings. There should be more simple, standardized disclosure modes, analogous to the standardized nutrition labeling on packages of food, that make it very easy for people to assess risks.

In his 2001 book *Republic.com,* legal scholar Cass Sunstein argued that the requirement for electronically disseminated disclosures, modeled after the SEC's, should be expanded to cover many other organizations whose activities could possibly affect the climate of our communications. The required disclosure of questionable activities can sometimes be enough to stop undesirable activities in their tracks. Sunstein wrote of the importance for a democratic republic of exposure to a broad spectrum of information: "To be sure, such a system depends . . . on some kind of public domain in which a wide range of speakers have access to a diverse public—and also to particular institutions and practices, against which they seek to launch objections."[*]

In our age of electronic communications, mandatory disclosure of information is more feasible than ever before. A business conduct regulator, such as proposed by Henry Paulson and his Treasury colleagues, could require mortgage lenders and other financial firms that interact with the general public to disclose on the Internet activities that appear questionable—such as predatory lending—thus opening them up to public scrutiny.

Improved Financial Databases

The fifth step toward an improved information infrastructure is for the government to subsidize the creation of large economic databases on both individuals and all firms, under a protocol that allows this information to be used to develop risk-management contracts and at the same time assures privacy.

We have already seen the development of large private databases of information on the incomes and economic activities of individuals, but these databases are fragmented and rarely used for good economic purposes. No one has the whole financial picture; only pieces are visible.

[*]Cass Sunstein, *Republic.com* (Princeton, N.J.: Princeton University Press, 2001), p. 201.

A protocol for the sharing of information among such databases needs to be developed, so that the current fragmented sources can be pooled. The enlarged pool of data should then be used for beneficial purposes, such as providing consumers and homeowners with more accurate pictures of their financial situations. Such enlarged databases would permit the financial engine web sites to offer customized, real-time information to their customers—information that relates to their particular circumstances.

Large publicly available databases of privacy-protected data on individual incomes are a real possibility, given that income taxes are now largely filed electronically. It is already possible for an individual in the United States to make information on his or her tax return available to financial counterparties by filing Form 4506-T. The government would of course have to take the next step, making identity-protected information appropriately and widely available for the public good. Other databases could be linked to the income database. This would permit, for example, the construction of an array of up-to-date and specific personal income indices by occupation, demographics, or health status. The data could then serve as the basis for the settlement of individually tailored risk-management contracts, such as the livelihood insurance described below. Risk-management engines could access the complete, fine-grained picture

would help prevent human error in economic thinking, which underlies many economic problems, including the subprime crisis.

Units of measurement would be defined for many common economic values, including income, profits, and wages. But of greatest importance would be new units of measurement for inflation.

I have been arguing for years that we can help avoid confused thinking about inflation by adopting an inflation-indexed unit of account, like the *unidad de fomento* (UF) that the government of Chile created in 1967 and that has since been adopted by other Latin American governments.

The UF is just the daily price of a market basket of goods and services, as measured by an interpolated Chilean consumer price index. But it has been singled out for publication by the government as a unit of account for commerce, replacing money. People in Chile commonly quote prices in UFs, although they still make actual payments in pesos using the peso-UF exchange rate (which is commonly available, in particular on a web site). By giving this unit of account a simple name, encouraging people to use it as a standard of value for commerce, and training them to think in indexed terms, its government has made Chile the most inflation-aware country in the world.

In contrast, the traditional currency units used by countries all over the world are a poor measure of value, since their buying power changes unpredictably over time. Measuring value in pesos or dollars is like measuring length with a ruler that expands or contracts from year to year. Engineers would find design a daunting task indeed with a meter rod that changed constantly—but that is exactly what people have to contend with when they deal in terms of money. No wonder they become confused. In the modern information-rich economy, there is no reason why the medium of exchange and the unit of value measurement need still be the same.

I would give these inflation-indexed units a simple name, *baskets,* to make clear that they represent the value of the market basket of goods and services upon which the consumer price index is calculated. If sellers name their prices in baskets, they are effectively asking to be paid in terms of the real goods and services that underlie the consumer price index—to be paid in real things rather than unstable currency. When we have a simple word to describe inflation-indexed quantities, even young children will learn to do inflation indexation, merely by using the word.

The government should write the tax code in terms of baskets, rather than dollars, to fully index the tax system and to force people to learn the new units. Credit card point-of-sale terminals and other electronic payment systems could be programmed to accept payments in baskets.

If people had become accustomed to such inflation-indexed units of measurement, the recent housing boom might have been averted. One of the most significant errors that have infected the housing market in recent decades has been the failure on the part of the general public to understand inflation. The governments of the major countries of the world have been publishing consumer price indices for nearly a century now, and the public at some level is able to use them. But confusion about inflation remains widespread and causes huge errors.

When U.S. inflation was very high, in the early 1980s, people could hardly afford to buy a home with conventional mortgages, since the inflation-zapped interest rates often approached 20% a year, and the purchase of a house worth just three years' income would entail mortgage payments approaching 60% of one's income. As inflation continued, mortgage payments would eventually come down dramatically in real terms, but that would not happen for years. Few could afford the early payments in those years, and so it became very difficult to buy a home. Home prices dropped, though the price drop was limited because there was an intense supply response to the high interest rates: residential investment as a share of U.S. GDP fell to 3.2%, the lowest point ever recorded in the period since World War II. All this could have been prevented if people had simply adopted inflation-indexed mortgages, but the public seemed unable to grasp the concept. Yet it would have been perfectly natural for them to do so had they already become accustomed to dealing in baskets.

The stock market was low in value in the early 1980s, reflecting the fact that nominal interest rates were very high, even though real (inflation-corrected) interest rates were not. This outcome is called the Modigliani-Cohn effect after the economists Franco Modigliani and Richard Cohn, who documented it in the late 1970s.

As inflation came down after the early 1980s, the stock market went up. This excessive movement of the stock market might have been prevented if accounting had been performed in terms of baskets, so that the public would have been less confused by so-called money illusion, the tendency to think of prices in nominal, not real, terms.

The housing boom since the 1990s is also due in part to the public's difficulty with understanding inflation. We remember home prices from long ago since they are such important purchases for us, and so the contrast between those prices and the prices today attracts our attention much more than the contrast between the price of a loaf of bread then and now. We get the false impression that homes have been a spectacular investment when in fact their increase in value, measured in baskets, even over many decades, would generally have been—at least until the recent housing boom—nil.

In 2008 the National Association of Realtors (NAR) launched a $40 million public awareness campaign entitled "Home Values." The campaign was designed to put thousands of advertising spots on radio and television, as well as ads in the print media, on billboards, and on bus shelters, These repeat the slogan "On average home values nearly double every ten years." The association claims that this statement is supported by their data for the past thirty years. Indeed it should be, for in the past thirty years consumer prices have nearly doubled twice, and we are at the end of a home-price bubble that caused real values to double once: that's three decades of doubling in nominal terms. It is deceptive to suggest from these data that homes will be spectacular investments, but the NAR can get away with it because of public confusion about inflation.

Indeed, even the Great Depression of the 1930s was intimately related to confusion about inflation. As Ben Bernanke points out in his 2000 book *Essays on the Great Depression,* it is now well known that, while prices in general were falling in the early 1930s, real wages (wages corrected for inflation) were high, and higher in countries that were harder hit by unemployment.

A simple story of the Great Depression is that employers could not cut the nominal wages of their workers enough to keep real wages constant, because cutting nominal wages would be misperceived by employees and their unions as a terrible insult, as an invitation to a fight. As a result, companies could not remain profitable while keeping their entire labor forces employed: their revenues would have fallen more than their costs did. The effects of the Great Depression would never have been as severe as they were if it weren't for confusion over inflation.

If people had been accustomed to quoting wages in baskets before the Depression, employees would have seen their real wages rising and presumably would not have had the same angry response to nominal wage cuts. Employers would not have had to shut down operations to remain solvent.

If we had been accustomed to quoting home prices in baskets since 1890, then people would generally have known that home prices haven't basically changed in a hundred years (until the recent bubble), and they would never have gotten the idea—as they did in the early 2000s—that home prices always go up.

Creating a new system of economic measurements would have countless other beneficial effects. In the context of some themes discussed earlier in this book, it is worth noting that we have allowed inflation (and income growth) to erode some of the important financial protections that were the product of enlightenment in years past.

When the Federal Deposit Insurance Corporation was created in 1934, the insured limit was $5,000—and this was twelve years' average per capita personal income. That limit was last raised in 1980, reflecting inflation and income growth, to $100,000. But $100,000 is less than three years' average per capita personal income today.

The insured limits of the Securities Investor Protection Corporation (SIPC), which protects customers when brokerage firms fail, were also last raised in 1980. They remain at $100,000 in cash accounts and $500,000 in securities—figures which may still sound large but which are not large enough to prevent panicked withdrawals by substantial numbers of brokerage customers should a major crisis ensue.

The erosion of these important protections has been compromising the resilience of our economic system. Defining the insurance limits of the FDIC and SIPC in nominal currency terms has been a serious design error. Defining the limits in terms of baskets would be better—and it would be even better to use another indexed unit of account tied to nominal personal income rather than inflation.

While the U.S. Congress has shown some inclination to make the appropriate fixes from time to time, as with the Federal Deposit Insurance Reform Act of 2005, the institutions remain seriously compromised by their lack of consistency. It is only through adopting a new system of economic units of measurement—so that correctly defining a quantity becomes as easy as saying a word—that we will avoid such mistakes in the future.

Information Infrastructure: A Summary

These six steps, taken together, would unleash the power of better information and help prevent economic crises like the current one from ever starting. Once we provide the economic and governmental incentives for the development of a better information infrastructure, and once that infrastructure has been in place for several years, then imagination and entrepreneurship will take over, pushing us into uncharted territory in the exploitation of that information. We will witness the creation of entirely new kinds of for-profit information providers, both computer-based and human-services-based, all interacting with each other to promote improved financial decision making by individuals and businesses.

New Markets for Risks That Really Matter

The history of finance over the centuries has been one of gradual expansion of the scope of markets. Over time, more and more kinds of risks are traded, and there are more and more opportunities for hedging those risks. Now is the time to encourage the further development of markets in a way that truly democratizes them, that is, so that the markets cover the specific risks that ultimately matter to individual people.[*]

New Markets for Real Estate

Most urgently needed is a truly liquid market for real estate, especially the single-family homes that constitute the single largest asset of most households.

I and my colleagues have been campaigning for innovative new markets for real estate for twenty years. Our big breakthrough came when the Chicago Mercantile Exchange (CME, now part of the CME Group, after its 2007 merger with the Chicago Board of Trade) created single-family home-price futures markets using the S&P/Case-Shiller Home Price Indices that Karl Case and I initially developed. These markets—spearheaded by Felix Carabello, John Labuszewski, and Anthony Zaccaria—were launched in May 2006 for ten U.S. cities

[*]A more extensive earlier development of these ideas for new markets is presented in Robert J. Shiller, *Macro Markets: Creating Institutions for Managing Society's Largest Economic Risks* (Oxford: Oxford University Press, 1993).

and for a composite U.S. index. They are the only true home-price futures markets in the world today. Despite efforts of market makers Jonathan Reiss and Fritz Siebel, liquidity in these markets is low, but we still have high hopes for them.

Such derivative markets have the potential to tame speculative bubbles in real estate. Without such markets, there is no way for investors to sell real estate short. There is no way for skeptical investors, who perceive that a bubble is in progress, to express this opinion in the market, except by actually getting out of the market, that is, selling their homes, which is of course a drastic and very difficult step.

If we *did* have a liquid market in real estate futures by city, then any skeptic anywhere in the world could, through his or her actions in the marketplace, act to reduce a speculative bubble in a city, for such a bubble represents a profit opportunity for short sellers. If the market were widely watched, then home builders would see the projected price declines and scale back their own activities, thus averting huge construction booms such as the one we have recently witnessed in the United States. If home builders adopted the enlightened practice of hedging their homes while they were still in production, then the losses would be felt before they even began building.

Some concerns have been expressed over the years that the creation of derivative markets might possibly *increase,* rather than decrease, the volatility of the underlying prices. However, according to a survey of the scholarly literature by financial economist Stewart Mayhew, "The empirical evidence suggests that the introduction of derivatives does not destabilize the underlying market—either there is no effect or there is a decline in volatility—and that the introduction of derivatives tends to improve the liquidity and informativeness of markets."[*]

The relevance of these findings to the market for homes is not entirely clear; the residential real estate market is exceptionally illiquid, and its prices are very salient to the broad public. However, in my mind, this is all the more reason to believe that introducing futures and bringing professionals into the market for homes will improve its functioning. Indeed, as economist Milton Friedman pointed out half a century ago, trading professionals ought to help stabilize markets at least to some extent, for if they are *destabilizing* markets (buying high and selling low), they are *losing* money—not a strategy that will keep them in business for long.

---

[*]Stewart Mayhew, "The Impact of Derivatives on Cash Markets: What Have We Learned?" Terry College of Business, University of Georgia, February 3, 2000, http://www.terry.uga.edu/finance/research/working_papers/papers/impact.pdf.

The prices in the CME housing futures markets have been predicting large declines in home prices in the United States almost since the markets' inception in May 2006. Had these markets been around and matured even earlier, well before 2006, and had they been widely known and understood, then the boom in construction whose consequences we now see would probably never have happened: builders would have seen the handwriting on the wall in the form of the authoritative price predictions that such markets generate.

Many substantial institutions see great potential in these futures markets. These markets could allow them to launch important retail risk management products, and then hedge the risks they acquire in doing so. But they also say that these markets are not really useful until they are liquid. They will not be liquid until the institutions start to trade. There is a "chicken and egg problem." To circumvent this, the futures markets need a catalyst to get the chickens together. The catalyst could result from some of the innovations to be described below, or from the exchange or from the government. The markets need an incentive for market makers to provide liquidity that in turn would draw other participants into the market.

Other kinds of markets for macro real estate risks include options, swaps, forwards, and similar derivative instruments. The CME launched an options market for single-family home prices in 2006, based on the S&P/Case-Shiller Home Price Indices, at the same time that it launched single-family home-price futures.

Pensions, endowments, and other global investors would find these markets, if they are liquid, fundamental to their activities. Real estate is a major asset class, comparable in size to the entire stock market, and should represent an important element of diversification for portfolio managers. An array of derivative markets would enable institutional investors to access this asset class in a more thorough and systematic way than they can today.

Commercial real estate is also starting to see such markets develop. The IPD indexes of commercial real estate in the United Kingdom have already seen the origination of over £15 billion of notional value. That is still quite small compared to the total value of commercial real estate in the United Kingdom, but it is an encouraging beginning.

Other New Markets

I place greatest emphasis on real estate markets in this book because real estate has been so important to business fluctuations, and particularly so in the current crisis. But there are many other kinds of new markets that need to be, and will be, created as we move to a more fully developed financial sector.

Foremost among these will be markets for long-term claims on incomes—individual incomes, incomes by occupation, incomes by region, and national incomes. These markets are important because they represent livelihood risk, the most important risk that each individual faces. Markets for occupational incomes—such as futures, forwards, swaps, and exchange-traded notes—will ultimately make it possible for people to hedge their lifetime income risks. The markets would be of fundamental importance for the issuers of continuous-workout mortgages, discussed below.

National incomes, sometimes measured by gross domestic product or GDP, deserve their own markets as well. These could in fact already exist, since GDP accounting is well developed, and data are maintained for every country in the world.

Stefano Athanasoulis and I have campaigned for governments to issue debt indexed to their GDPs. Stephany Griffith-Jones and Inge Kaul at the United Nations Development Program, Eduardo Borensztein and Paolo Mauro at the International Monetary Fund, and Kristin Forbes at the Council of Economic Advisors, have also advocated such ideas. This could be perpetual debt that pays a share of GDP as dividend. My colleague Mark

Kamstra of York University, who has been working with me to promote the adoption of such government securities in Canada, has suggested calling these trills, since it would be natural to have each share pay a trillionth of a year's GDP. This would mean that one Canadian trill would be currently paying an annual dividend of about CA$1.50, and one U.S. trill would be paying an annual dividend of about US$15.00.

These dividends would go up or down through time depending on the level of economic success of the country. The market price of one Canadian trill might today be in the vicinity of CA$30, and that of one U.S. trill roughly US$300. The price of a trill would fluctuate with information about the future prospects of the country, just as a company's stock price fluctuates with information about the future prospects of the company. Presumably there would be a lively and interesting market for these securities.

Most importantly, a market for trills would allow countries to hedge their national economic risks. If the U.S. government had issued trills over the years, and if a substantial fraction of the national debt were trills, then the U.S. government would find that it had freed up sufficient resources to allow it to deal promptly with an emergency like the subprime crisis. In an economic slowdown, the government would find that the burden of interest on the national debt would, in effect, fall below expectations.

It would thus have more resources available to deal with the crisis. That is fundamental risk management, applied on a national scale.

Of course trills have never yet been issued by any government. There have been some GDP-linked securities, notably Argentina's issue in 2005 of GDP warrants. To establish these better, further work should be done on improving the timelines and replicability of GDP numbers, and reducing the tendency for substantial subsequent revisions.

New Retail Risk-Management Institutions

The new markets described above are intended to create a general infrastructure for risk management. But the general public cannot be expected to use sophisticated risk-management techniques. For example, most people will never trade in futures markets: they are not accustomed to doing so, and such trading poses significant challenges to the uninformed. For them we need to design simple retail products that will allow them to participate in these new markets, thus truly achieving the democratization of finance.

The analogy is to the kind of risk management that grain elevators provide to individual farmers. Farmers do not generally hedge their risks on futures markets; that is often too difficult a strategy for the individual farmer. But a farmer will sign a contract for delivery of his grain to the local grain elevator, and that contract pushes some of the farmer's market risk to the owner of the elevator— who will in turn hedge the risk in the futures markets.

That simple concept is a model for vastly improved risk management for individuals. Retail organizations can channel the benefits of the risk markets described above to individuals.

Continuous-Workout Mortgages

A new kind of home mortgage that I call a *continuous-workout mortgage* would have terms that are adjusted continuously (in practice probably monthly) in response to evidence about changing ability to pay and changing conditions in the housing market. The mortgage contract would schedule an automatic workout every month— much as is currently done on a one-time-only basis during the mortgage workouts offered to defaulting homeowners. Continuous-workout mortgages would be privately issued, and the government would be involved only in providing appropriate regulation and infrastructure.

One type of continuously adjusted mortgage made its appearance as far back as the high-inflation, high-interest-rate period of the late 1970s to the early 1980s.

The price-level-adjusted mortgage (PLAM) advocated by Franco Modigliani allowed payments to respond monthly to changes in a single economic indicator: the inflation rate as measured by the consumer price index. Today we can do much better than the PLAM, for the consumer price index would be only one of many factors to be taken into account in any mortgage workout.

The continuous-workout mortgage would exemplify the democratization of finance since the benefits of such mortgages would naturally accrue to *everyone*. The workouts would be systematized and automated, so that they would land in the laps of all who could appropriately benefit from them—not just those who were savvy about finding a good lawyer, proactive in asserting their rights, or prone to arousing sympathy as conspicuously needy.

I argued in the last chapter that bailouts of some sort are a necessary part of the subprime solution, to avoid an economic crisis that would destroy public confidence and possibly lead to systemic failure. Unfortunately, such bailouts have a side effect: they encourage moral hazard. People may act irresponsibly because they come to *expect* bailouts. But this side effect is a serious problem only when the bailouts are neither arranged in advance nor freely chosen by all parties. If people pay in advance, in a free market, for the right to a bailout, then it is no longer a bailout; it is an insurance policy. If it nevertheless encourages undesirable behavior, it is at least undesirable behavior whose costs have been covered.

Continuous-workout mortgages are one way of providing for a "responsible" bailout. These financial devices, set up in advance, would do what bankruptcy courts do on an emergency basis after the fact: they would adjust the terms of a loan to the borrower's ability to pay. But, unlike bankruptcy proceedings, continuous-workout mortgages operate on an ongoing basis, responding to fluctuations in income as they occur and not allowing problems to build up to crisis level. Think of them as regular checkups and preventive care rather than a sudden trip to the emergency room. Nor do they entail the embarrassment and loss of reputation associated with a bankruptcy. Indeed continuous-workout mortgages continue to function under circumstances that otherwise would trigger a bankruptcy claim, allowing the lender to continue collecting a stream of payments that, while perhaps reduced, is at least uninterrupted.

There remains of course a potential moral hazard with continuous-workout mortgages: a borrower might deliberately lose his job in order to trigger reductions in loan payments or, worse yet, work in the shadow economy and not report any income. Moral hazard is inherent in all risk management, including insurance and bankruptcy, and risk-management institutions can, with sufficient diligence, reduce it to manageable levels. Dealing with moral hazard is likely to be much more effective if the responses to income loss are planned in advance, rather than as part of an ad hoc bailout, by risk-management institutions that have an incentive to contain moral hazard.

One way to structure continuous-workout mortgages to reduce moral hazard is to write into the loan contract a payment formula that relies not only on the borrower's actual income but also on indicators of the earning ability of others in the same geographic area and occupational category. Under such a plan, a borrower could intentionally reduce her own income, but this would not have much effect on the payment schedule, since she could not influence the other indicators. So-called occupational income indices, if designed properly, could achieve the ideal of loan terms truly dependent on ability to pay while minimizing moral hazard.

Continuous-workout mortgages clearly ought to be a central pillar of any plan to deal with the subprime crisis. The fact that mortgage workouts are now being advocated so strongly, and by people of so many political persuasions, implies that the workouts should be institutionalized, regularized, and made permanent. Continuous-workout mortgages do just that.

Home Equity Insurance

Decreases in home values can reduce or even eliminate a homeowner's equity, making it difficult or impossible for the owner to refinance with a new mortgage. The homeowner may conclude that it is impossible to move to another home, even if such a move would allow her to take advantage of a lucrative job offer. The mortgage may eventually end in default, especially since the homeowner may decide that it is just not worth struggling to make further payments on a mortgage when she can just walk away from the whole mess.

Home equity insurance contracts can be written on the market values of homes in a metropolitan area, protecting homeowners against declines in the value of their homes within their local markets. Home equity insurance would eliminate the risky, often highly leveraged, position in which so many homeowners find themselves today. Such contracts would go a long way toward preventing many homeowners from ever falling into negative equity positions, thus allowing them to remain in their homes. This in turn would foster the various social and psychological benefits of homeownership, encouraging the maintenance of neighborhoods and promoting civic participation.

With fire insurance, there is always the moral hazard that a homeowner will deliberately burn down the home in order to collect on the insurance. If we wrote home equity insurance policies directly on the selling prices of homes, then we would have an analogous moral hazard: the homeowner would lose any incentive to maintain the home properly or to negotiate the best price on its sale. Any loss would be incurred by the insurance company. But if the insurance is written on the aggregate value of the homes in a city, rather than on the value of an individual home, then there is no moral hazard.

Home equity insurance would also eliminate the panic selling that sometimes devastates housing values, when owners see home prices starting to fall and decide to bail out. Had such insurance contracts been available in the past, we might not have seen the collapse of home values in major cities undergoing racial change, and the transitions could have been smoother and gentler than the "white flight" that actually occurred—a sort of negative speculative bubble built, in that case, around a racial story. The economic destruction of neighborhoods in such cities as Detroit, Philadelphia, and Washington might have been minimized or perhaps avoided altogether. Had city centers remained vital, industry might have been more inclined to remain in place, further supporting the vitality of the cities.

Home equity insurance has been tried before. The first attempt took place in Oak Park, Illinois, in 1977. An important recent experiment, in the city of Syracuse, New York, was carried out by some of my colleagues at Yale, with the help of the Neighborhood Reinvestment Corporation. This pilot program was innovative in that it was based on a home-price index for the city of Syracuse rather than on the selling price of the individual homes, thereby controlling moral hazard.

The concept of home equity insurance can also be implemented, essentially, through options. The options for single-family home prices now traded at the CME offer a clear route that homeowners can use today to protect themselves against the risk of falling home prices tomorrow. Anyone can buy a put option on home prices at the CME, which acts like an insurance policy that pays off if home prices fall below the strike price of the option.

These put options are available to the general public today, but few avail themselves of them, let alone have any appreciation of the financial theory of risk sharing that lies behind them. Options are widely thought of by the public as financial gimmicks for reckless investors, when in fact they are effective devices for spreading and canceling risks. But skepticism has always greeted the introduction of new investment vehicles in the retail marketplace, and properly conducted programs of education will eventually allow the general public to understand and benefit from the concepts of real estate options.

Livelihood Insurance

Today, when a middle-aged person loses a steady job, as when an industry shuts down or the demand for that person's services drops, it may lead to a loss of income that becomes a crushing lifetime disaster. Louis Uchitelle, in his 2007 book *The Disposable American: Layoffs and Their Consequences,* discovered that those on whom this misfortune falls are truly suffering—but suffering mostly in silence, out of a sense of shame and of being at fault.

Livelihood insurance would be a significant step toward addressing the consequences of job loss. It would build on another existing risk-management institution: disability insurance. But it would expand its coverage beyond just *medical* risks to take account of *economic* risks to livelihood as well.* When disability insurance was

---

*Livelihood insurance was proposed, and the concept developed, in Robert J. Shiller, *The New Financial Order: Risk in the 21st Century* (Princeton, N.J.: Princeton University Press, 2003).

invented, the level of information technology was such that medical risks to ability to earn an income were sufficiently measurable and verifiable to allow insurance policies to be written on those risks. But disability insurers of the time had no reliable way of measuring economic effects on an individual's livelihood. Today we have sophisticated econometric indices of livelihoods based on large databases—and these indices can and no doubt will be improved even further over time.

To avoid moral hazard, livelihood insurance cannot of course simply guarantee a specified level of income to the insured, lest that individual stop working and begin living off the insurance settlement. But—in parallel with continuous-workout mortgages and home equity insurance—it ought to be possible to write livelihood insurance policies whose payouts are connected only partly, if at all, to the insured's own income, while still insuring against specific risks to that income. Occupational income indices appropriate to an individual's line of work could be used to define an insured loss without inducing moral hazard. If there were markets for occupational income risk, then a private insurer could hedge the risk it was incurring by writing such policies.

The existing disability insurance industry provides a natural infrastructure upon which to build livelihood insurance.

Livelihood insurance might be viewed as a more modern and effective embodiment of the concept of unemployment insurance, a century-old concept. When unemployment insurance was invented in the United Kingdom in 1911, and implemented under the leadership of David Lloyd George, *The Times* of London wrote, "But for the unemployment scheme there is no precedent. It is really a 'leap in the dark,' and an uncommonly bold one."* The gamble on the new scheme paid off. Over time unemployment insurance has been copied all over the world, and the entities that provide it have largely been able to keep moral hazard under control. Yet unemployment insurance in its present form never really managed to insure long-term livelihoods effectively.

Given our much-improved information technology and more sophisticated financial theories, we should be able to advance the mission first taken up by the framers of unemployment insurance. Because of the complexity of its implementation, livelihood insurance should probably be offered by private insurance companies, facilitated by the government through regulation, infrastructure, and support of associated public goods, such as education.

---

*"Unemployment Insurance," *The Times*, May 13, 1911, p. 11.

The subprime crisis coincides with a time of transition for many people into, if not permanent unemployment, then permanent loss of the ability to earn substantial income for the rest of their lives. Livelihood insurance would go a long way toward mitigating the effects of such a trend. This time of crisis—when millions stand to undergo transitions to significantly reduced circumstances over their lifetimes—is the ideal time to consider it.

Risk Management versus Risk Avoidance

The adoption of risk-management devices like those discussed above would have fundamental effects. When we lack such devices, we tend to avoid risks in less optimal ways. Risk-avoidance behavior can, for example, have undesirable consequences for our decisions about where we work and live. Unable to insure against the risks inherent in our choice of geographic area, we may tend to choose safe jobs that we think we can never lose. We may elect to work in large metropolitan areas, where a wide variety of job opportunities are available, rather than in small rural communities or towns far from city centers, where the job markets are likely to be more specialized. Thus we tend to be more conventional in our choice of occupations and more dependent on big cities and their suburbs than we may want to be.

Risk-avoidance behavior also has an impact on the behavior of city, regional, and even national governments. Fearing the uncertainties associated with new economic development initiatives, these governments typically choose to play it safe and model themselves along conventional lines. They slavishly imitate other successful entities when they ought to be cultivating their locales as vital centers for specific emerging technologies or industries.

The result of all this avoidance behavior is a depressing uniformity and lack of adventure in our society. People should certainly avoid essential risks—risks to society at large—but not necessarily *insurable* risks, which can be spread out across large segments of the population and thereby blunted. But people tend to avoid both kinds of risks, draining society of much of its creativity and vitality.

What If? The Combined Effect
of the Elements of a Long-Term Solution

Imagine our society equipped with a well-established information infrastructure that reached out to all its members; derivative markets for both owner-occupied and commercial real estate; well-developed retail products, like continuous-workout mortgages, home equity insurance, and livelihood insurance, that facilitate risk management for individuals; and default options that naturally lead people to use risk-management devices intelligently.

The crazily inefficient pricing in the market for owner-occupied homes would come to an end. The exaggerated swings of home prices, reflecting speculative thinking, would be tempered by the market actions of international investors and thus would be far less likely to cause the kind of disruptions we have been seeing in the current subprime crisis. A major source of business instability, fluctuations in real estate investment, would be rationalized.

Our society could look forward to nothing less than more stable markets and, in turn, a more rational economy. We would eventually find ourselves forgetting that the kind of massive financial instability infecting our everyday lives is even a potential problem. Modern finance, applied democratically, can relegate these problems to history just as modern medicine, applied widely, has left us forgetting that epidemics of yellow fever and diphtheria ever raged among us.

Epilogue

7

The key to long-term economic success is rightly placed confidence in markets. In contrast, bubbles are the result of misplaced confidence.

The various components of the subprime solution described in this book are designed to facilitate such rightly placed confidence, by making the markets and their associated risk-management institutions work as they ideally can, for the benefit of all of us.

The short-term component of the solution described here is the most urgent. People are suffering and businesses are collapsing. The memories of these traumas will harm confidence and trust in our markets for years to come, just as they did during the Great Depression. With each passing day more damage is done to our social fabric.

But the long-term component of the subprime solution is also ultimately needed to consolidate our stabilization. We must seize the opportunity today to make changes that will allow everyone to participate in the construction of a better future. The process of economic development is not over—we are learning from the current crisis, and the changes we make now can lead to a permanently better world.

The long-term solution that I have offered here may strike some as rather unexpected. Suggesting as it does the further development of our financial markets and institutions, freeing them to work better, the solution may seem to be moving us in exactly the wrong direction.

Indeed, there are some who argue that the whole financial sector has been in a bubble, which will eventually burst. According to labor economists Thomas Philippon and Ariell Reshef, the U.S. financial sector has grown from 2.3% of GDP in 1950 to 7.7% of GDP in 2005. Some of this rapid growth is likely due to the booms in stock, housing, oil, and other commodities markets over the last twenty years.

But Philippon and Reshef also show that there has been a marked shift within the financial sector since the late 1970s: In the 1970s, financial workers were only slightly more educated and received only slightly higher wages than other workers. Since then the skill intensity and remuneration of financial workers has grown much faster than in the economy at large.* It seems clear that this change reflects the growth of an important emerging technology of finance. Recognizing this, the next logical step is to assure that this technology becomes available for the benefit of everyone.

There are those who imagine that the entire solution to the subprime crisis is in either sidestepping or punishing the financial sector. They think that the solution is to be found in more bailouts, regulations, rules, penalties, and prison sentences.

I too have argued that, in the short term, bailouts should indeed play some role in our response to the crisis. Whenever the economic system is discovered not to have insured people properly, bailouts are a sign of our attentive humanity for each other.

Our sense of trust in each other is itself substantially the legacy of former humane actions that at times took the form of bailouts. Consider the Marshall Plan, which was in a sense a gift from the United States to the damaged nations of Europe after World War II. The payments were not made in fulfillment of any prearranged

*Thomas Philippon and Ariell Reshef, "Skill Based Financial Development: Education, Wages and Occupations in the U.S. Financial Sector," National Bureau of Economic Research Working Paper No. 13437, September 2007, http://www.nber.org/papers/w13437.

insurance contract. They were the embodiment of the principles that Keynes had laid out in his *Economic Consequences of the Peace* a generation earlier. They were humane responses to the terrible situation in which Europe found itself after the war. In his 2006 book *How to Cure a Fanatic,* novelist and social critic Amos Oz claimed that "It was the Marshall Plan that won the cold war. Not ray guns and star wars, but the Marshall Plan. I think that communism was defeated through the Marshall Plan, though its overthrow took thirty or forty years more to realize. It was Harry Truman, not Ronald Reagan, who won the cold war through the Marshall Plan."[*]

We can only hope that some of the same generosity toward those who have been ill treated will appear again in the current financial crisis.

But we cannot go forward with an assumption that ad hoc bailouts will be an appropriate mechanism for protecting human economic and social welfare in the future. The same moral premise that underlies bailouts today requires that we get to work to set up systematic procedures to deal *in advance* with comparable future crises.

We must *institutionalize* generosity to the unfortunate. Doing so ultimately means producing risk-management contracts. Doing this is a natural extension of the trend in

---

[*]Amos Oz, *How to Cure a Fanatic* (Princeton, N.J.: Princeton University Press, 2006), p. 79.

our society, over the past two hundred years, of replacing many of our charitable institutions with insurance-based institutions.

Are people less grateful when the reimbursement they receive is a payout of an insurance policy rather than an act of charity? Probably. But gratitude is not our objective here. Close on the heels of gratitude may come a sense of shame and personal failure. Social stability, lack of discord, is enhanced most of all by a general sense that we have institutions that treat all of us in a fair and compassionate way, even though the actions of these institutions do not require any spontaneous impulse to generosity.

The aftermath of the subprime crisis has involved considerable finger-pointing, It is natural to want to blame what has happened on some combination of evildoers. The danger is that the emphasis on placing blame may cause us to lose sight of the real solution.

Of course, there *have* been evildoers. Every financial boom creates opportunities for the unscrupulous among us, and the opportunities demand that they hide behind a veil of corporate correctness, which makes their behavior all the more galling after the truth is known. During the subprime crisis, some of them had been especially insufferable, with their self-interested claims that there was no problem in the housing market, arguing with each successive month that the market would bottom out in the next month or so. It is easy to feel little sympathy with these people after the dénouement.

It is no surprise that the heads of some of the biggest investment banks and broker-dealers have now been fired; the person at the helm is frequently let go, if only to symbolize hopes for a new beginning. But we do not want to let our desire for retribution go beyond this, to the punishment of the institutions themselves and their principles.

The reaction to the stock market crash of 1929 and the resulting Depression led to considerable anger in parts of Europe, and intense nationalism and racism. That led to a further weakening of the continent's financial system. In contrast, in the United States in the 1930s, the reaction to the 1929 financial crisis was to try to strengthen our financial sector. The mistaken venting of European hostility on smoothly functioning financial markets was fully appreciated only half a century later. We need to maintain this financial enlightenment.

A related, parallel development complicates the issue: for several decades there has been a steady rise in economic inequality in the United States, as well as in most of the developed nations of the world. With each passing year, the continued worsening of that inequality further strains our tolerance of those who make large amounts of money in the financial markets.

But this should not be an occasion for punishing the *technology* that has created the riches—for finance is indeed a powerful technology, and it can be a powerful means for making everyone better off. It can even be used to *reduce* economic inequality. A good deal of the economic inequality in the modern world is due to the persistence of unmanaged risks, and financial technology is ideally suited to deal with these risks.

It is true that the rise in inequality has in part been due to cronyism on corporate boards, whose members have increasingly felt that top managers are entitled to exorbitant levels of compensation. But we should not assume that this is the main cause of the rise in inequality, and it certainly does not suggest that waging war on the financial elite is the best way to deal with the problem.

I believe that in many cases it is true that top executives in the world of finance are not the most caring people—or at least that they are in less caring stages of their lives, caught up as they are in the game of finance, too filled with the competitive spirit and too busy to think about the needy. Clearly they are not nurses or kindergarten teachers. But public policy directed against their activities is not the solution to our problems.

It may be difficult, in the present climate of public anger directed at our financial markets, for political candidates to win support on the promise of expanding and developing our financial markets. But that is exactly what is needed now to solve the subprime crisis and prevent a recurrence of similar economic crises in the future.

Index